S0-AER-468

VERY EASY TOEIC® Second Edition
Beginning TOEIC® Test-taking Skills

Beginning TOEIC® Test-taking Skills

VERY EASY
TOEIC®

Second Edition

Anne Taylor
Garrett Byrne

Schaumburg Township District Library
130 South Roselle Road
Schaumburg, IL 60193

Compass
Publishing

2/14
ENCOMIUM
#23

ABE
C
428
TAYLOR,A

3 1257 01939 6851

VERY EASY TOEIC® Second Edition
Beginning TOEIC® Test-taking Skills

Anne Taylor • Garrett Byrne

© 2007 Compass Publishing

All rights reserved. No part of this publication may be reproduced, stored in a retrieval system or transmitted in any form, or by any means, electronic, mechanical, photocopying, recording or otherwise, without prior permission in writing from the publisher.

TOEIC is a registered trademark of Educational Testing Services (ETS).

Acquisitions Editor: Garrett Byrne
Development Editor: Emily Page
Recording Manager: Wendy Oh
Recording Assistant: Elisa Ha
Cover/Interior Design: Dammora Inc.

Email: info@compasspub.com
http://www.compasspub.com

ISBN: 978-1-59966-024-0

10   09   08   07
10   9   8   7   6   5   4   3   2

PHOTO CREDIT

JupiterImages Corporation: (© 2005 Photos.com)
IMSI MasterPhotos: (© 1997)

CONTENTS

At a Glance

	Vocabulary		Grammar Focus	Preposition
	Listening	**Reading**		
Unit 1	frown/yawn/cry/laugh nod/act/clap/kiss	though/through already/yet sometime/sometimes	Present Tense	at
Unit 2	pay/sell/try on/shop return/count/shake/lend	borrow/lend appointment/promise be used to/used to	Past Tense	in
Unit 3	stretch/ride/swim/play row/dance/make/kick	fun/funny mind/remind get on/take	Gerunds / Infinitives	from
Unit 4	work/wrap/build/design measure/serve/deliver/type	by/until during/for employee/employer	Subject-Verb Agreement	to
Unit 5	say/call/chat/shout talk/yell/speak/whisper	bring/take advice/advise say/tell	Auxiliaries	by
Unit 6	point/raise/write/wave hug/help/cheer/show	affect/effect another/other when/while	Relative Pronouns	with
Unit 7	feed/chew/have/eat pour/cook/bring/give	desert/dessert a few/a little any/some	Nouns / Pronouns	for
Unit 8	hop/jump/chase/load play/fix/march/fly	almost/most hard/hardly late/lately	Adjectives / Adverbs	into
Unit 9	clean/wash/cut/comb sweep/fold/polish/check	fewer/less object/subject raise/rise	Comparisons	on
Unit 10	sing/paint/play/watch take a bath/lie/read/relax	quiet/quite interested/interesting lay/lie	Conjunctions	over
Unit 11	stand/hide/get up/wait look/listen/wear/rest	either/too look/seem hear/listen	Modifiers	about
Unit 12	walk/throw/water/climb pick/gather/dig/park	explode/explore wander/wonder afford/effort	Negation	of

Preface

Very Easy TOEIC® Second Edition has been designed for beginning-level students of English who need to start preparation for the TOEIC®.

This book contains twelve units, one practice test, and support with a transcript and answer key. Each unit in this book contains a vocabulary section, a clear and concise grammar focus section, grammar exercises, and a Mini Test.

Vocabulary

A. Listening: With simple listening practice, students study vocabulary frequently appearing on the TOEIC®.
B. Reading: Pair exercises help students distinguish between commonly confused words.

Grammar Focus and Exercises

This part outlines fundamental grammar points frequently tested on the TOEIC®. Each unit begins with a brief explanation of the target grammar, including key points. The units also provide exercises based on the format of TOEIC® grammar questions, allowing students to practice their understanding of the grammar point.

Mini Test

This section provides a mini test that incorporates the same types of questions as the latest TOEIC® format. With this, students can not only review the grammar learned in Grammar Focus and Exercises but also become familiar with the kind of tasks they will encounter on the TOEIC®.

Practice Test

The Practice Test provides students with an opportunity to take a full-length, lower-level version of a TOEIC® test. It introduces students to the new TOEIC® format, incorporating 100 listening questions and 100 reading questions.

Support — Transcript, Answer Key

The Support includes reference materials related to the above chapters, including a transcript for all listening tasks in each unit and in the practice test, an answer key for each unit and the practice test, and a blank sample answer sheet for use when taking the full-length practice test.

Introduction

About TOEIC®

TOEIC® stands for Test of English for International Communication. It is divided into two main sections: Listening and Reading. The Listening section tests the ability to understand spoken English. The Reading section tests the knowledge of grammar and vocabulary and the ability to read and understand short passages.

There are a total of 200 questions on the TOEIC® test, and the test lasts about two hours. All of the items are multiple-choice questions with three or four possible answers. The following chart outlines the organization of the test as of May 2006:

Organization of the TOEIC®

Section 1: Listening Test

Part 1:	Picture Description	10 questions
Part 2:	Questions and Responses	30 questions
Part 3:	Short Conversations	30 questions
Part 4:	Short Talks	30 questions
Listening Total		100 questions
		45 minutes

Section 2: Reading Test

Part 5:	Incomplete Sentences	40 questions
Part 6:	Incomplete Texts	12 questions
Part 7:	Reading Comprehension	48 questions
Reading Total		100 questions
		1 hour 15 minutes

Grand Total	**200 questions**	**2 hours**

LISTENING TEST

In this section of the test, you will have the chance to show how well you understand spoken English. There are four parts to this section, with special directions for each part.

Part 1   **Picture Description**

The directions for Part 1 of the TOEIC® appear on the test as follows:

Directions: In this part of the test, you will hear four statements about each picture in your textbook. After listening to all four statements, you must select the one statement that best describes what you see in the picture. Then, find the number of that question on your answer sheet and mark your answer. The statements will be spoken only one time, and are not printed in your test book.

Look at the sample below.

Now listen to the four statements.

(A) The woman is using a musical instrument.
(B) The woman is typing on a computer.
(C) The woman is playing a video game.
(D) The woman is sitting behind the table.

Sample Answer

(A) ● (C) (D)

Statement (B), "The woman is typing on a computer," best describes what you see in the picture. Therefore, you should choose answer (B).

TIPS

- Preview the picture before the statements are read. Ask yourself, "Who?" "What?" "Where?"
- Focus on the meaning of the statements as a whole.
- Answer the question as quickly as possible. If you don't know the answer, guess and begin previewing the next picture.

TRICKS

- Incorrect answers may contain similar sounding words.
  e.g. The woman is tying on a computer.
- Incorrect answers may give wrong pronouns, numbers, and locations.
  e.g. He is typing on a computer. / There are two computers. / The woman is sitting under the sofa.
- Incorrect answers may include a correct word.
  e.g. The computer is for sale. / The woman is sitting with some friends.

9

The directions for Part 2 of the TOEIC® appear on the test as follows:

> **Directions:** In this section you will hear a question or statement followed by three responses. Select the best response to the question or statement and mark the letter (A), (B), or (C) on your answer sheet. Again, each response will be spoken only one time and will not be printed in your test book.
>
> Now listen to the four statements.
>
> You will hear:
> Good morning, John.
> How are you?
>
> You will also hear:
> (A) I'm fine, thank you.
> (B) I'm in the living room.
> (C) My name is John.
>
> Sample Answer
>
>
> The best response to the question "How are you?" is choice (A), "I'm fine, thank you." Therefore, you should choose answer (A).

TIPS

- The first word of the question will help you to know what kind of answer is required.
  What, where, who, why, how—ask for information.
  Do, does, did, are, is, will, can—usually need a yes/no answer.

- Questions that contain "or" and require a choice never have yes/no answers.
  "Did you stay home or go out last night?" "I went to a movie."

- Sometimes you will hear a statement, not a question. However, it still requires an answer.
  "Thanks for dinner." "You're welcome."

TRICKS

- Pay attention to words that sound the same (homonyms).
  e.g. two, too, to

- Look out for tag questions that are added to the end of statements.
  e.g. "That movie was great, wasn't it?"

- Watch out for indirect answers. Sometimes the answer to a yes/no question does not include the words "yes" or "no."
  e.g. "Is there enough gas in the car?" "I just filled it yesterday."

Part 3　Short Conversations

The directions for Part 3 of the TOEIC® appear on the test as follows:

> **Directions:** In this section of the test, you will hear a number of conversations between two people. You will be asked to answer three questions about what is said in each conversation. You must select the best response to each question and mark the letter (A), (B), (C), or (D) on your answer sheet. Each conversation will be spoken only one time and will not be printed in your test book.

TIPS

- Look at the question before the dialog begins. If you have time, look at the answers as well.
- While you are listening to the dialog, try to imagine where the speakers are.
- Read all the answers before making your choice.

TRICKS

- Watch out for answers that are true, but not related to the question. Don't answer too quickly. Read all the options before you choose.
- Watch out for distracting numbers. These may include dates, times, and numbers of things or people. Preview the question to help you listen for the right information.

Part 4　Short Talks

The directions for Part 4 of the TOEIC® appear on the test as follows:

> **Directions:** In this section of the test, you will hear a number of short talks given by a single speaker. Again, you must answer three questions about what is said in each talk. Choose the most appropriate response to each question and mark the letter (A), (B), (C), or (D) on your answer sheet. Each talk will be spoken only one time and will not be printed in your test book.

TIPS

- Listen closely to the introduction preceding the talk. It will tell you the number of the questions related to the talk. It will also tell you what type of information you will hear (news report, weather report, advertisement, recorded message, announcement, etc.).
- Try to preview the questions before the talk begins. This will help you listen for the information required by the questions.
- Begin to answer the questions as soon as the talk is finished. Don't wait for the speaker.

TRICKS

- Watch out for the same traps that are in Parts 1-3.

READING TEST

In this section of the test, you have a chance to show how well you understand written English. There are three parts to this section, with special directions for each part.

Part 5   Incomplete Sentences

The directions for Part 5 of the TOEIC® appear on the test as follows:

> **Directions:** In each question, you will find a word or phrase missing. Four answer choices are given below each sentence. You must choose the best answer to complete the sentence. Then mark the letter (A), (B), (C), or (D) on your answer sheet.
>
> *Example*:
> Because the equipment is very delicate, it must be handled with -------.
> (A) caring
> (B) careful
> (C) care
> (D) carefully
>
> Sample Answer
>
>
> The sentence should read, "Because the equipment is very delicate, it must be handled with care." Therefore, you should choose answer (C).

TIPS

- Don't worry about spelling. Incorrect spelling is never an option in TOEIC® answers.
- Look at the words on either side of the blank. They can give you clues about what the correct answer is.
- Read the whole sentence and understand the meaning before you answer.

TRICKS

- Watch out for answers with the wrong word form.
  e.g. drove, drives, driving
- Watch out for words that use the same beginnings or endings.
  e.g. return, retire, reuse
- Watch out for commonly misused words.
  e.g. affect/effect, lend/borrow

The directions for Part 6 of the TOEIC® appear on the test as follows:

Directions: Read the text on the following pages. You will find a word or phrase missing in some of the sentences. Below each of the sentences, four answer choices are given. Select the most appropriate answer to complete the text. Then mark the letter (A), (B), (C), or (D) on your answer sheet.

Example:

As of June 15th, employees will be ------- to wear full company uniform whenever

    1. (A) requiring
        (B) requirement
        (C) required
        (D) require

they are on company premises. This ------- to all employees who work in areas of

    2. (A) considers
        (B) applies
        (C) works
        (D) implements

Sample Answer			
1. Ⓐ	Ⓑ	●	Ⓓ
2. Ⓐ	●	Ⓒ	Ⓓ

the building accessible by members of the public. The full uniform consists of a white shirt, green pants, and the company tie for men.

The sentences should read "As of June 15th, employees will be required to wear full company uniform whenever they are on company premises. This applies to all employees who work in areas of the building accessible by members of the public." Therefore you should choose answers (C) and (B).

TIPS

- Remember that you are looking for the most appropriate word to fill in the blank.
- Read the whole text, not just the words around the blank. Try to get the meaning of the text.

TRICKS

- Watch out for repetition and redundancy
  e.g. keep on continuing, finally at last
- Watch out for words that don't belong
  e.g. The apples they are fresh.
- Pay attention to word form and verb tenses
  e.g. nice/nicely, had gone/has gone

The directions for Part 7 of the TOEIC® appear on the test as follows:

Directions: In this part of the test, you will read a selection of texts, such as magazine and newspaper articles, letters, and advertisements. Each text is followed by several questions. Choose the correct answer to each question and mark the letter (A), (B), (C), or (D) on your answer sheet.

Read the following example.

The Grenville Museum Of Technology is a "hands-on" museum, designed for people to experience science at work. Although this kind of museum may be fairly common nowadays, Grenville was the first of its kind in the United States. Visitors are encouraged to use, test, and handle the various objects on display. Special demonstrations are scheduled for the first and second Wednesday of each month at 13:30. The museum is open Tuesday-Friday 12:00-16:30, Saturday 10:00-17:30, and Sunday 11:00-16:30. Admission is $2 for children and $3 for adults.

At what times during the month can visitors see special demonstrations?
(A) Every weekend
(B) The first two Wednesdays
(C) One afternoon a week
(D) Every other Wednesday

Sample Answer
 Ⓐ ● Ⓒ Ⓓ

The reading says that the demonstrations are scheduled for the first and second Wednesdays of the month. Therefore, you should choose answer (B).

TIPS

- As with Part 4, pay attention to the introduction. It will tell you the number of questions and a hint about the type of information in the passage.
- As you read the passage, ask yourself, "Who is it for? Why was it written?"
- First, glance quickly through the passage and read the questions. Then, go back to the passage and try to look for the answers to the questions.

TRICKS

- Many answers use information that appears in the passage. However, they may not directly answer the question.
- As with all sections of the TOEIC®, watch out for similar sounding words, confusing numbers, wrong word forms, and words with similar meanings.
- Don't be confused by questions that follow these formats:
  e.g. Which of the following is NOT mentioned in the reading?
      The text refers to all of the following EXCEPT . . .
- Simply read the answer choices and find the one that is unfamiliar or incorrect.

Present Tense

Vocabulary

A. LISTENING (Expression)

Listen and write the letter of the statement that best describes the picture.

Exercise 1

1. _____ 2. _____ 3. _____ 4. _____

Exercise 1
1. (D) Frown   2. (A) Yawn
3. (B) Cry   4. (C) Laugh

Exercise 2

1. _____ 2. _____ 3. _____ 4. _____

Exercise 2
1. (D) Nod   2. (C) Act
3. (B) Clap   4. (A) Kiss

B. READING (Commonly Confused Words)

Choose the correct word to complete each sentence.

Exercise 1

1. They walked (though / through) the mud.
2. (Though / Through) it was raining, they went outside.

Exercise 1
1. through   2. Though

Exercise 2

1. I have (already / yet) finished my homework.
2. She has not finished her homework (already / yet).

Exercise 2
1. already   2. yet

Exercise 3

1. (Sometime / Sometimes), I like to walk in the park.
2. (Sometime / Sometimes) tomorrow, I will paint the fence.

Exercise 3
1. Sometimes   2. Sometime

Present Tense

1. Simple present

The simple present is frequently used with *always, sometimes, usually, often, rarely, hardly, ever, never.*

▶ **Use the simple present for routines, habits, or statements that are always true.**

a) The Earth is round.
b) I usually get up at 7:00 in the morning.

▶ **Use the simple present for future events that are certain to take place.**

a) He comes back tomorrow.
b) When does the train leave?

> **Note** You can also use the present progressive for future events that are certain to take place.

a) He's coming back tomorrow.

2. Present perfect

Present perfect verbs are often used with *once, twice, -times, ever, never, finally, just, already, yet, recently.*

▶ **Use the present perfect (have/has + past participle) to describe an action that happened in the past, where the time of the action may not necessarily be known.**

a) I have been to the United States.
b) We have lived here for twenty years.
c) John has seen the movie twice.
d) I have just finished the project.

3. Present progressive

Present progressive verbs are frequently used with *this week, today, at the moment, for the time being, currently.*

▶ **Use the present progressive (is/are + -ing) for an action that is currently in progress.**

a) I'm eating lunch right now.
b) What are you talking about?

> **Note** Stative verbs do not occur in the progressive tense.

Stative verbs include *know, own, belong, have, like, hate, seem, appear, hear, smell, taste, see, resemble*

a) I'm having a pen. (X) → I have a pen.
b) She's seeing a bird. (X) → She sees a bird.

4. Present perfect progressive

▶ **Use present perfect progressive verbs (has/have been + -ing) for situations that began in the past and are continuing in the present.**

a) He has been calling her all morning.
b) It's been raining here since we arrived.

Usage

at school
at 7:30
at first
at the target

At

a) He works at night.
b) I got up at 6:00 this morning.
c) She lives at 123 Main Street.

Grammar Exercises

Choose the correct word or phrase to complete each sentence.

Hint

1. Every morning, I (am going / go) to school at eight o'clock.

    every morning

2. Mina (studies / has studied) French for ten years.

    for ten years

3. I have not (saw / seen) him since 1995.

    since 1995

4. I (am having / have) three dogs.

    ----

5. The baby has (been crying / cries) all day.

    has, all day

6. Mr. Gray sometimes (plays / is playing) tennis.

    sometimes

7. Look! A mouse (runs / is running) through the door.

    Look!

8. What are you (study / studying) at school tomorrow?

    are you, tomorrow

9. Have you (finish / finished) your homework yet?

    have, yet

10. Father is (laughing / laughs) at the movie.

    is

Part 1 Picture Description

Listen and choose the statement that best describes the picture.

1.   (A)   (B)   (C)   (D)

2.   (A)   (B)   (C)   (D)

3.   (A)   (B)   (C)   (D)

4.    (A)   (B)   (C)   (D)

5.   (A)   (B)   (C)   (D)

Listen and choose the correct answer.

1.   (A)   (B)   (C)
2.   (A)   (B)   (C)
3.   (A)   (B)   (C)
4.   (A)   (B)   (C)
5.   (A)   (B)   (C)

Listen and choose the correct answer.

1. What feature does the man mention?

    (A) The woman's height   (B) The woman's age
    (C) The woman's face   (D) The woman's hair

2. What is the woman doing?

    (A) She is fixing the photocopier.
    (B) She is using the fax machine.
    (C) She is making photocopies.
    (D) She is taking photos.

3. Which sentence is true?

    (A) Mary doesn't know the woman.
    (B) The photocopies are ready.
    (C) The woman is a new employee.
    (D) The man wants to make photocopies.

---

4. Why does the woman have a headache?

    (A) The room is very large.
    (B) The room is dark.
    (C) The man doesn't want to work.
    (D) The woman works too hard.

5. What warning does the man give the woman?

    (A) She must use less electricity.
    (B) She should relax more often.
    (C) She should not use a computer every day.
    (D) She should turn on the lights.

6. Who had a similar problem?

    (A) The man   (B) The man's sister-in-law
    (C) The man's sister   (D) The woman's sister

Listen and choose the best answer to each question.

1. Which of the following takes the longest time to get to the speaker's workplace?

    (A) The subway
    (B) The bus
    (C) The bike
    (D) The taxi

2. How long does it take the speaker to walk to the subway station?

    (A) Ten minutes
    (B) Fifteen minutes
    (C) Twenty minutes
    (D) Fifty minutes

3. How does the speaker get to work in the winter?

    (A) By bus
    (B) By train
    (C) By taxi
    (D) By bike

4. What is the woman's job?

    (A) Designing cakes
    (B) Making wedding dresses
    (C) Planning weddings
    (D) Arranging flowers

5. Why is today an amazing day for the woman?

    (A) It is the woman's birthday.
    (B) It is her sister's birthday.
    (C) It is the woman's wedding.
    (D) She is planning her sister's wedding.

6. Which of the following is NOT true?

    (A) The woman designed a cake.
    (B) The woman will wear a nice dress.
    (C) The guests will dance.
    (D) The woman will get married.

Choose the word or phrase that best completes the sentence.

1. Our family ------- in this city for twenty years.

    (A) having live   (B) is living
    (C) has lived   (D) live

2. Paul and I are ------- to the movies.

    (A) go   (B) going
    (C) goes   (D) gone

3. The car ------- to my uncle.

    (A) belongs   (B) belong
    (C) are belonging   (D) belonging

4. I eat lunch ------- school every day.

    (A) once   (B) now
    (C) twice   (D) at

5. The train goes ------- many tunnels.

    (A) though   (B) at
    (C) through   (D) yet

6. She ------- yawns in English class.

    (A) sometimes   (B) already
    (C) sometime   (D) though

7. We ------- to London three times.

    (A) going   (B) go
    (C) have been   (D) have went

8. The bus ------- every twenty minutes.

(A) run   (B) runs
(C) are running   (D) running

9. I ------- to watch comedies on TV.

(A) liking   (B) likes
(C) am liking   (D) like

10. She ------- on the phone since I came in.

(A) has been talking   (B) talks
(C) talked   (D) talking

11. They ------- at two o'clock tomorrow.

(A) arrived   (B) have arrived
(C) are arriving   (D) have been arriving

12. I've ------- the book already.

(A) will read   (B) read
(C) reading   (D) been read

13. He ------- a lot of money with him.

(A) is having   (B) has
(C) have   (D) had had

14. They've ------- all weekend.

(A) study   (B) been study
(C) studies   (D) been studying

15. She's ------- for the singer.

(A) clap   (B) claps
(C) clapping   (D) been claps

Choose the best word or phrase for each blank.

<u>Questions 1 through 3</u> refer to the following memo.

To: All employees

From: Management

This is a reminder about the next general meeting. There will be a meeting for employees **1.** ------- 9:30 a.m. on Wednesday, June 25th.

       (A) on
       (B) in
       (C) at
       (D) by

All employees must attend. Please **2.** ------- John Fisher in the payroll office if you

       (A) notify
       (B) talk
       (C) repeat
       (D) speak

cannot attend. If you have not told him **3.** -------, please tell him before Tuesday

       (A) now
       (B) since
       (C) yet
       (D) though

afternoon. The meeting will be held in the main conference room.

Questions 4 through 6 refer to the following letter.

Dear Mrs. Jones,

Thank you for your letter of May 15th. I am very sorry that the handle of your new pan broke. I have **4.** ------- asked our supplies office to replace your pan.

(A) yet
(B) soon
(C) already
(D) ago

We **5.** ------- every product very carefully, but, as with every large company,

(A) buy
(B) check
(C) sell
(D) have

6. ------- a faulty product does pass through. I apologize for the inconvenience.

(A) sometime
(B) sometimes
(C) ever
(D) even

Please enjoy the $50 gift voucher attached to this letter. I hope you will continue to shop at Headway Hardware.

Sincerely,
Alex Morgan
Quality Control
Headway Hardware

Choose the best answer.

<u>Questions 1 and 2</u> refer to the following chart.

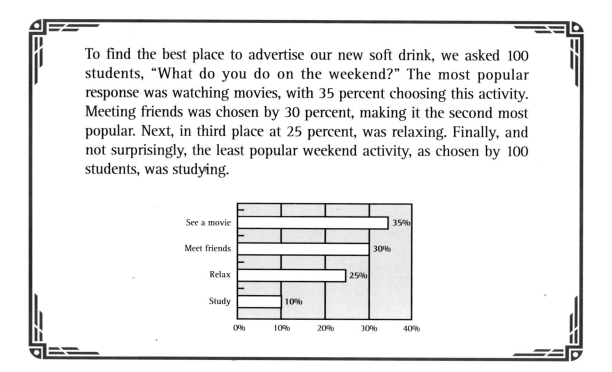

To find the best place to advertise our new soft drink, we asked 100 students, "What do you do on the weekend?" The most popular response was watching movies, with 35 percent choosing this activity. Meeting friends was chosen by 30 percent, making it the second most popular. Next, in third place at 25 percent, was relaxing. Finally, and not surprisingly, the least popular weekend activity, as chosen by 100 students, was studying.

1. What was the most popular response?

   (A) Seeing a movie   (B) Meeting friends
   (C) Relaxing   (D) Studying

2. How many students study on the weekend?

   (A) 25%   (B) 20%
   (C) 15%   (D) 10%

Questions 3 through 5 refer to the following advertisement.

Try new and improved Green Mountain Tea. Traditionally grown and hand picked by the folks who have developed tea for centuries, Green Mountain Tea gives you a taste of history. It's delicious, and it's healthy, too. Green Mountain Tea contains more vitamins than any other tea on the market.* Good for colds, headaches, and even stomachaches! One box of fifty tea bags is only $5.00.

* Note — claim not yet proven through scientific study

3. Which of the following is NOT true?

(A) Green Mountain Tea is delicious.
(B) Green Mountain Tea is good for toothaches.
(C) Green Mountain Tea is good for headaches.
(D) Green Mountain Tea is new.

4. How many tea bags are in one box?

(A) Twelve   (B) Twenty
(C) Fifteen   (D) Fifty

5. How much does it cost for one tea bag?

(A) $5.00   (B) $0.50
(C) $0.10   (D) $1.00

Questions 6 through 9 refer to the following chart and letter.

Peter's Diet (kilograms)

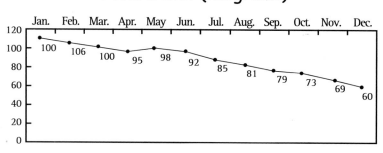

At the beginning of the year, I decided to lose weight. In January and February, I began swimming twice a week in order to burn off some calories. In May, I spent a week in Mexico and gained back some of this lost weight by eating too many tacos. In the summer, I began eating more vegetables instead of meat. Twelve months later, I feel quite satisfied with my weight loss.

6. How much did Peter weigh in May?

(A) 98 kg   (B) 95 kg
(C) 93 kg   (D) 90 kg

7. How much did Peter weigh at the end of the year?

(A) 110 kg   (B) 40 kg
(C) 60 kg   (D) 75 kg

8. How often did Peter go swimming?

(A) Twice a week   (B) January
(C) For two months   (D) For twelve months

9. Where did Peter gain weight?

(A) At the gym   (B) In May
(C) In Mexico   (D) On his coffee break

Past Tense

Vocabulary

A. LISTENING (Transactions)

Listen and write the letter of the statement that best describes the picture.

Exercise 1

1. _____   2. _____   3. _____   4. _____

Exercise 1
1. (B) Pay   2. (D) Sell   3. (C) Try on   4. (A) Shop

Exercise 2

1. _____   2. _____   3. _____   4. _____

Exercise 2
1. (A) Return   2. (C) Count   3. (D) Shake   4. (B) Lend

B. READING (Commonly Confused Words)

Choose the correct word to complete each sentence.

Exercise 1

1. George (borrowed / lent) some money from the bank.
2. Will you (borrow / lend) me a pen?

Exercise 1
1. borrowed   2. (D) lend

Exercise 2

1. He has a(n) (appointment / promise) this afternoon.
2. The politician made a(n) (appointment / promise) to the people to cut taxes.

Exercise 2
1. an appointment
2. a promise

Exercise 3

1. I will never (get used to / used to) the cold weather here.
2. She (is used to / used to) live by the sea when she was young.

Exercise 3
1. be used to   2. used to

Grammar Focus

Past Tense

1. Simple present

   ▶ **Use the simple past tense for an action that was finished in the past.**

   a) We went shopping yesterday.
   b) Columbus discovered America in 1492.
   c) I lent you fifty dollars two days ago.
   d) She ate dinner before we went to the movie.

   Note Use *used to* for an action that was repeated or occurred regularly. Use *would* for actions that were repeated, though irregular.

   a) I used to play soccer with my friends when I was young.
   b) I would listen to music while studying for final exams in high school.

2. Past perfect

   ▶ **Use the past perfect tense (had + past participle) for an action that occurred before a certain point in the past.**

   a) She had bought the book before I met her.
   b) He had been to Oxford twice before I went there.

   Note *Before* can be used in a simple past and past perfect sentence.

   a) I cleaned the house before she visited.
      (= I cleaned the house because I knew she would visit.)
   b) I had cleaned the house before she visited.
      (= I cleaned the house, and, by coincidence, she visited after I had cleaned.)

3. Past progressive

   ▶ **Use the past progressive tense (was/were + -ing) for an action that was in progress when a second past action took place (or when a second past action was also in progress.)**

   a) When Jackie got there, Steve was waiting for her.
   b) While I was taking a bath, Sally was using the computer.

4. Past perfect progressive

   ▶ **Use the past perfect progressive tense (had been + -ing) to show an action that was in progress for a known length of time and was still in progress when some other action occurred.**

   a) He said he had been doing his homework since six o'clock.
   b) They had been cleaning the room for an hour already when I walked in.

Preposition

Usage

in the evening
in spring
in the box
in a month

In

a) I used to live in a house.
b) He went to Austria in 2002.
c) She'll arrive in an hour.

Choose the correct word or phrase to complete each sentence.

1. He didn't go shopping because he (is / was) sick.

    didn't go

2. Mr. Lee (have sold / sold) his house two months ago.

    two months ago

3. I (took / was taking) a shower when the phone rang.

    when the phone rang

4. I (used to / am used to) play in the park when I was young.

    when I was young

5. He (finished / finish) the work before I got there.

    before I got there

6. Shirley (had been waiting / waited) for twenty minutes when he arrived.

    when he arrived

7. While I was talking on the phone, she (was reading / reads) magazines.

    while

8. Jenny said she had already (return / returned) the movie.

    already

9. He (borrowed / had borrowed) money from me three days ago.

    three days ago

10. He (had been waiting / waited) in the station since 2:00 when the train finally arrived.

    since

Listen and choose the statement that best describes the picture.

1. (A)   (B)   (C)   (D)

2. (A)   (B)   (C)   (D)

3. (A)   (B)   (C)   (D)

4.   (A)   (B)   (C)   (D)

5.   (A)   (B)   (C)   (D)

Part 2 Questions and Responses

Listen and choose the correct answer.

1. (A)   (B)   (C)
2. (A)   (B)   (C)
3. (A)   (B)   (C)
4. (A)   (B)   (C)
5. (A)   (B)   (C)

Listen and choose the correct answer.

1. Which sentence is true?

   (A) The man and woman were classmates.
   (B) The man and woman have met before.
   (C) The man and woman have never met before.
   (D) The woman wants to buy some shoes.

2. Where did the man and woman meet first?

   (A) In his shoe store
   (B) In the woman's house
   (C) In the man's house
   (D) In a department store

3. What did the man use to do?

   (A) He worked in a department store.
   (B) He owned his own store.
   (C) He was an actor.
   (D) He had a lot of shoes.

---

4. Which sentence is true?

   (A) The man was in his office all day.
   (B) The man missed a meeting.
   (C) The man met Eric.
   (D) The man made a phone call.

5. Why was the man late?

   (A) He woke up late.
   (B) He had car trouble.
   (C) The traffic was bad.
   (D) His watch was broken.

6. What will the man probably do next?

   (A) Take the subway
   (B) Telephone Eric
   (C) Call the woman
   (D) Take a break

Listen and choose the best answer to each question.

1. How often does this company have a staff picnic?

   (A) Every month   (B) Every year
   (C) Twice a year   (D) Every Christmas

2. Which of the following will NOT be available at the picnic?

   (A) A barbecue   (B) Drinks
   (C) Games   (D) A movie

3. Which prizes are mentioned?

   (A) A holiday and a CD player
   (B) A DVD player and a CD player
   (C) A DVD player and a holiday
   (D) A holiday and a television

4. Why does the speaker want to be a doctor?

   (A) To help sick people
   (B) To earn lots of money
   (C) To work in a hospital
   (D) To study at university

5. How long was the speaker's mother in the hospital?

   (A) One week   (B) Two weeks
   (C) Three weeks   (D) Four weeks

6. What does the speaker say about being a doctor?

   (A) It's expensive.   (B) His mother is a doctor.
   (C) It's hard work.   (D) You don't have to study much.

Choose the word or phrase that best completes the sentence.

1. When I arrived at my aunt's home, she ------- her kitchen floor.

    (A) was sweeping   (B) sweep
    (C) had sweeping   (D) sweeps

2. His dog ------- outside in the rain all day yesterday.

    (A) has been   (B) was been
    (C) been   (D) was

3. I ------- about the funny story before he told me.

    (A) have heard   (B) had heard
    (C) hear   (D) was hearing

4. Joseph told me he ------- his project.

    (A) already finishes   (B) finishing
    (C) had already finished   (D) had been already finishing

5. It ------- for two days when I arrived in town.

    (A) rained   (B) rains
    (C) has been raining   (D) had been raining

6. She ------- to Canada on Saturday.

    (A) flying   (B) has flying
    (C) is flying   (D) has been flying

7. My teacher told us that the school ------- in 1946.

    (A) was building   (B) was built
    (C) has been built   (D) is built

8. He sometimes ------- money from his parents.

(A) lend

(B) borrow

(C) lends

(D) borrows

9. She always ------- the expensive shoes.

(A) try on

(B) tries on

(C) trying on

(D) had tried on

10. Lynn ------- her dog when I saw her in the park.

(A) was walking

(B) walked

(C) have been walking

(D) walking

11. I ------- very angry yesterday, so I didn't talk to him.

(A) am

(B) had been

(C) have been

(D) was

12. Yesterday, I met a friend, saw a movie, and ------- home late.

(A) coming

(B) have come

(C) came

(D) had come

13. There used to be ten students ------- my class.

(A) at

(B) on

(C) to

(D) in

14. The traffic is very heavy, but I think we'll get there ------- six o'clock.

(A) before

(B) on

(C) ago

(D) in

15. The robbers ------- the money when the police arrived.

(A) count

(B) counting

(C) are counting

(D) were counting

Choose the best word or phrase for each blank.

<u>Questions 1 through 3</u> refer to the following email.

To: david_brian@gomail.net
From: ephughes@soreteeth.net
Re: Cancellation of Appointments

Dear Mr. Brian,

You **1.** ------- not come to your appointment on January 5th. In the future, please let us

    (A) were
    (B) had
    (C) did
    (D) are

know if you need to cancel **2.** ------- . Please try to call at least five hours before your

    (A) a promise
    (B) a meeting
    (C) an appointment
    (D) an arrangement

appointment time, so that we can give it to another **3.** ------- . Thank you for your

    (A) patience
    (B) patients
    (C) patient
    (D) patent

assistance.

Sincerely,

Everett Hughes

Questions 4 through 6 refer to the following notice.

New Opening Hours

Sun Valley Shopping Mall customers: please note our new opening hours.

As you know, we **4.** ------- open at 8.30 a.m. on weekdays, and at 10 a.m. on

        (A) are used to
        (B) used to
        (C) had to
        (D) wanted to

weekends. **5.** ------- January 31st, we are opening at 10 a.m. every day. Last year,

      (A) On
      (B) At
      (C) In
      (D) From

we had few customers before 10 a.m., so we decided to change our hours. We are sorry for this change, but **6.** ------- that shopping at the mall will be even more fun.

        (A) say
        (B) try on
        (C) promise
        (D) let

Look out for some special events and offers coming soon!

Choose the best answer.

<u>Questions 1 and 2</u> refer to the following advertisement.

Used Computer For Sale

Pentium 4 — only 3 years old

- Includes 19-inch LCD monitor, 40X CD/DVD combination drive, 256 MB of memory, and a 40-GB hard drive.
- Comes with a color printer-scanner combo, surround sound speakers, and a super-fast wireless Internet connection.
- Can be yours for only $350. Call Steve at 568-1974 (after 6:00 p.m.) or at 574-4791 (from 9:00 a.m. - 5:00 p.m.).

1. How old is the computer?

   (A) Four years old
   (B) Three years old
   (C) Two years old
   (D) One year old

2. What is offered with the computer?

   (A) A monitor
   (B) A telephone
   (C) A refrigerator
   (D) A desk

Questions 3 through 5 refer to the following advertisement.

Hamburger House

Summer Special Offer!

That's right, we've brought back our annual Summer Special Offer here at Hamburger House.

Buy two juicy hamburgers ⇨ get one hamburger free!
Buy two giant cheeseburgers ⇨ get one cheeseburger and one drink free!

Cool off with a Mountain Milkshake (Caramel or Raspberry) for only $1.50 or a Glacier Sundae (Blueberry or Double Chocolate) for only $2.50.

The Summer Special Offer will last all summer, from June 1st to August 31st!

3. If you buy two giant cheeseburgers, what do you get free?

(A) Two hamburgers and a drink
(B) One cheeseburger and one drink
(C) Two cheeseburgers and a drink
(D) One cheeseburgers and two drinks

4. How long does the offer last?

(A) All year
(B) All month
(C) Three months
(D) Three weeks

5. How often does this special offer happen?

(A) Every year
(B) Once a month
(C) Not very often
(D) Twice a year

Wanted: Private Chinese Tutor

My husband, two children, and I need a Chinese teacher because we are moving to Hong Kong next summer. The teacher must come for one hour on Monday, Wednesday, and Thursday evenings. We have some background in Chinese vocabulary and grammar, so we need to focus our classes on writing and conversation. We are willing to pay $20 an hour to the right person. Email Deb at chinafan@mailnet.com.

To: chinafan@mailnet.com
From: lilywong@chinmail.net
Subject: Tutor
Date: August 30th

Dear Deb,

I am a Chinese teacher from Hong Kong. I am now a student here in New Zealand. I taught Chinese in my home country, so I have a lot of experience. I am free every evening. I am very interested in meeting you and your family.

Please call me on 09-993-444

Lily Wong

6. Who wrote the advertisement?

(A) The husband   (B) The wife
(C) The children   (D) The teacher

7. Why do they need a teacher?

(A) They are moving to another country.
(B) They are taking a trip to Hong Kong.
(C) They are Chinese.
(D) They have two children.

8. How much do they want to pay per week?

(A) $20   (B) $30
(C) $40   (D) $60

9. What did Lily Wong do before she moved to New Zealand?

(A) She was a student.   (B) She was a teacher.
(C) She was free every evening.   (D) She lived in Hong Kong.

Gerunds / Infinitives

Vocabulary

A. LISTENING (Leisure I)

Listen and write the letter of the statement that best describes the picture.

Exercise 1

1. _____   2. _____   3. _____   4. _____

Exercise 1
1. (C) Stretch   2. (A) Ride
3. (B) Swim   4. (D) Play

Exercise 2

1. _____   2. _____   3. _____   4. _____

Exercise 2
1. (D) Row   2. (A) Dance
3. (B) Make   4. (C) Kick

B. READING (Commonly Confused Words)

Choose the correct word to complete each sentence.

Exercise 1

1. Soccer is (fun / funny) to play.
2. The comedian is (fun / funny).

Exercise 1
1. fun   2. funny

Exercise 2

1. Would you (mind / remind) rowing for a while?
2. Please (mind / remind) me to stretch before I exercise.

Exercise 2
1. mind   2. remind

Exercise 3

1. Sue (gets on / takes) the bus to school.
2. Hold my books while I help the lady (get on / take) the bus.

Exercise 3
1. takes   2. get on

Gerunds / Infinitives

1. Use the -ing form after the following verbs: avoid, deny, enjoy, finish, give up, mind, spend.

   a) I enjoyed working at the restaurant.
   b) Finally, she gave up smoking.

2. Use a to-infinitive after the following verbs: agree, decide, expect, fail, hope, want.

   a) He agreed to join our soccer team.
   b) I want to travel to the moon some day.

3. Use a to-infinitive after the following verbs plus their objects: allow, ask, expect, tell, want, would like.

   a) My boss told me to finish the project by next Monday.
   b) She asked her husband to stop smoking.

4. Use the -ing form after the following verb phrases: look forward to, get used to, object to, can't help, can't stand.

   a) I look forward to hearing from you soon.
   b) We can't help having more cookies. They're delicious!

5. After the following verbs, the to-infinitive and -ing forms have the same meaning: begin, hate, like, prefer, start.

   a) It began to rain. = It began raining.
   b) I like to ride a bike. = I like riding a bike.

6. After the following verbs, the to-infinitive and -ing forms have different meanings: try, remember, forget.

   a) He remembered to call his friend.
   b) He remembered calling his friend.

7. Use the -ing form when using go + verb constructions with the following verbs: camp, hunt, skate, dance, jog, swim.

   a) All our class went camping last weekend.
   b) I would like to go fishing this Saturday.

8. Use only the -ing form after a preposition.

   a) They talked about studying together.
   b) I am interested in traveling to France.

P r e p o s i t i o n

from my grandmother
from Ireland
from 1:00 to 2:00
from the start

From

a) I got a watch from my father.
b) Peter got back from his trip to Hong Kong.
c) We work from 9 a.m. to 6 p.m.

Choose the correct word or phrase to complete each sentence.

1. We gave up (going / to go) on a picnic because of the heavy rain.

    gave up

2. He asked her (helping / to help) him with his homework.

    asked, him

3. James wanted (traveling / to travel) to Europe by himself.

    wanted

4. They look forward to (seeing / see) their son next month.

    look forward to

5. I'm planning to go (swimming / to swim) with my friend Bill tomorrow.

    go

6. Please remind me (buying / to buy) some milk.

    remind

7. Janet spent $200 (buying / buy) a new cell phone.

    spent

8. Would you like me (getting / to get) something to eat on my way back from work?

    like

9. My father has recently stopped (smoking / to smoke) due to his health problems.

    stopped

10. These days, you can buy almost anything without (going / to go) to the store.

    without

Part 1 Picture Description

Listen and choose the statement that best describes the picture.

1.  (A) (B) (C) (D)

2. (A) (B) (C) (D)

3.  (A) (B) (C) (D)

4.

(A)　　(B)　　(C)　　(D)

5. 　　(A)　　(B)　　(C)　　(D)

Listen and choose the correct answer.

1. 　(A)　　(B)　　(C)

2. 　(A)　　(B)　　(C)

3. 　(A)　　(B)　　(C)

4. 　(A)　　(B)　　(C)

5. 　(A)　　(B)　　(C)

Listen and choose the correct answer.

1. What are the man and woman discussing?

   (A) A new car   (B) Their manager

   (C) New curtains   (D) A meeting

2. What color did the manager select?

   (A) Green and yellow   (B) Yellow

   (C) Blue   (D) Green

3. Why does the man think it is a good idea?

   (A) The curtains will make the room look brighter.

   (B) The room will be less stressful.

   (C) Blue curtains are less expensive.

   (D) The room will look bigger.

4. What is the woman doing?

   (A) Searching for something on her desk

   (B) Looking for something

   (C) Drinking coffee

   (D) Looking for someone

5. Where does the man think the glasses are?

   (A) At home   (B) On the woman's desk

   (C) In the woman's car   (D) In the kitchen

6. What does the woman remember?

   (A) The man's birthday

   (B) Where she left her car

   (C) That her glasses are in her car

   (D) That her keys are on her desk

Listen and choose the best answer to each question.

1. Why was the concert postponed?

   (A) Flooding   (B) Not enough seats
   (C) Damaged lights   (D) A sick singer

2. How much would five tickets cost?

   (A) One hundred dollars   (B) Fifty dollars
   (C) Twenty dollars   (D) Two hundred dollars

3. How many tickets in total are available?

   (A) 500   (B) 200
   (C) 400   (D) 1000

4. Which three languages is the speaker studying?

   (A) English, Spanish, and German (B) Spanish, German, and French
   (C) French, English, and German (D) English, Spanish, and French

5. Why does the speaker have a lot of chances to speak Spanish?

   (A) The speaker is French.   (B) The speaker went to Spain on a vacation.
   (C) The speaker is Spanish.   (D) The speaker has a Spanish-speaking friend.

6. Which language is the most difficult for the speaker?

   (A) English   (B) French
   (C) Spanish   (D) German

Choose the word or phrase that best completes the sentence.

1. We all look forward ------- you very soon.

   (A) to see   (B) to seeing
   (C) will see   (D) like seeing

2. She enjoys ------- in her free time.

   (A) swim   (B) to swim
   (C) swims   (D) swimming

3. I ------- you to clean your room yesterday.

   (A) remind   (B) reminded
   (C) mind   (D) minded

4. Last weekend, we went horseback ------- on the farm.

   (A) ride   (B) rode
   (C) riding   (D) ridden

5. My back is sore because I forgot ------- before I exercised.

   (A) to stretch   (B) stretching
   (C) stretched   (D) stretch

6. My wife ------- work at the GoodAll Company.

   (A) was   (B) used to
   (C) was accustomed to   (D) interested in

7. The actress was tired of ------- autographs.

   (A) sign   (B) signature
   (C) signs   (D) signing

8. Several students from the suburbs ------- buses to school.

(A) get on
(B) getting on
(C) take
(D) taking

9. The manager ------- us to return the DVD before noon today.

(A) likes
(B) is liking
(C) would like
(D) liked

10. Why haven't you ------- your hair yet?

(A) comb
(B) combed
(C) to comb
(D) combing

11. I can't come to the party because I'm going -------.

(A) shop
(B) shopped
(C) shops
(D) shopping

12. My boss told me ------- the project by this Friday.

(A) finish
(B) to finish
(C) finishing
(D) to finishing

13. That new student in class is ------- Japan.

(A) at
(B) on
(C) in
(D) from

14. It is difficult ------- from England to France.

(A) row
(B) rowed
(C) to row
(D) row to

15. I don't have time ------- for the cheapest car.

(A) look
(B) looked
(C) to look
(D) looking

Choose the best word or phrase for each blank.

Questions 1 through 3 refer to the following message.

Message

Jane,

Frank Green called while you were out. He wants you to **1.** ------- him back as soon

                                          (A) tell
                                          (B) say
                                          (C) call
                                          (D) yell

as you get this **2.** ------- . He has met with the employees, and he would like to

            (A) ad
            (B) writing
            (C) document
            (D) message

3. ------- the schedule for the staff sports day. He says he has some good ideas. He

(A) talk
(B) discuss
(C) speech
(D) speak

is looking forward to talking to you.

Questions 4 through 6 refer to the following email.

To: bestdresses@hmm.com
From: Alice Carter <acarter@hmm.com>
Subject: Delivery
Date: August 2ⁿᵈ

Hi Sally,

I just wanted you to know about the delivery of cotton for the dresses you are making. I'm sorry for the delay, but it is now ready to **4.** ------- . It will arrive about

(A) buy
(B) lend
(C) send
(D) make

1 p.m. on Friday, August 6ᵗʰ. I **5.** ------- to the supplier, but he denied receiving the

(A) complained
(B) suggested
(C) returned
(D) telephoned

order. In fact, I had to place the order again, but this time there were no problems. Please let me know if it does not arrive on Friday. I hope you are **6.** ------- the

(A) fun
(B) amusing
(C) pleasure
(D) enjoying

summer weather.

Sincerely,

Alice Carter

Choose the best answer.

Questions 1 and 2 refer to the following note.

Andrea,
This note is just to remind you of what needs to be done today. I'm very busy from early this morning until late in the afternoon, so I don't have time to do all this.

1. Wash the car
2. Mail this letter
3. Pay the gas bill
4. Pick up my clothes from the dry cleaner's
5. Return the videos we watched last night
6. Make a pizza for dinner tonight

Thanks so much!
Casey

1. Where will Andrea probably NOT go?

    (A) To the post office   (B) To the theater
    (C) To the dry cleaner   (D) To the car wash

2. Why does Casey ask Andrea to do these things?

    (A) Because he's tired   (B) Because he's sick
    (C) Because he's not home   (D) Because he's busy

Questions 3 through 5 refer to the following chart.

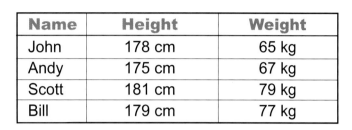

Name	Height	Weight
John	178 cm	65 kg
Andy	175 cm	67 kg
Scott	181 cm	79 kg
Bill	179 cm	77 kg

John and his three friends decided to join the army. When they went to the army office, the army doctor began checking their height and weight. John was a bit embarrassed because he was thin and weighed only 65 kg. Andy was also embarrassed because he was the shortest. After the doctor's check up, the boys began training.

3. Who checked their height?

(A) John   (B) Andy
(C) The doctor   (D) Bill

4. Who was embarrassed?

(A) John and Scott   (B) Bill and Scott
(C) Andy and the doctor   (D) Andy and John

5. Why did John and his friends go for a check up?

(A) Because John was sick
(B) Because they were sick
(C) Because they wanted to join the army
(D) Because John is a doctor

Questions 6 through 9 refer to the following poster and email.

JOIN OUR CLUB!

Do you like to act, sing, and dance? Would you like to meet a new group of friends as dramatic as you are? If so, then please join our performers' club. We meet every Wednesday evening from seven o'clock to nine o'clock at the Clark City Community Center. We can promise you a great night! Everyone is welcome. We look forward to seeing you there! Email us at performclub@stagenet.com.

To: performclub@stagenet.com
From: MGreen@happnet.net
Subject: Performers' Club
Date: September 13th

I would like to join the performers' club because I love singing, acting, and dancing. However, I am worried that my singing and dancing are not good enough. Is it OK to join even if I am not very good? Please let me know.

Thank you,
Mary Green

6. Who can join the performers' club?

(A) Anyone   (B) Only men
(C) Only women   (D) No one

7. How long do club meetings last?

(A) Once a week   (B) Two hours
(C) At seven o'clock   (D) On Wednesday evening

8. How often do they meet?

(A) Every day   (B) Three times a week
(C) Twice a week   (D) Once a week

9. Why is Mary Green worried?

(A) She can't find the community center.
(B) She is not a good singer.
(C) She is very dramatic.
(D) She is not good at meeting new people.

Subject – Verb Agreement

Vocabulary

A. LISTENING (Work)

Listen and write the letter of the statement that best describes the picture.

Exercise 1

1. _____   2. _____   3. _____   4. _____

Exercise 1
1. (B) Work   2. (D) Wrap
3. (A) Build   4. (C) Design

Exercise 2

1. _____   2. _____   3. _____   4. _____

Exercise 2
1. (D) Measure   2. (C) Serve
3. (A) Deliver   4. (B) Type

B. READING (Commonly Confused Words)

Choose the correct word to complete each sentence.

Exercise 1

1. He finished his homework (by / until) ten o'clock.
2. She worked (by / until) nine o'clock last night.

Exercise 1
1. by   2. until

Exercise 2

1. I fell asleep (during / for) the movie.
2. She will stay in Europe (during / for) two weeks.

Exercise 2
1. during   2. for

Exercise 3

1. The boss is the (employee / employer).
2. The worker is the (employee / employer).

Exercise 3
1. employer   2. employee

Grammar Focus

Subject–Verb Agreement

singular	plural
is / has	are / have
every, each more than one many a	a number of, a couple of a group of, kinds of a few, several many, both all of, most of

John and I = we
John and Mary = they

1. Use singular verbs after the names of countries and (singular) subjects that finish with -s.

   a) The United States has a population of over 265 million people.

   b) Mathematics is my favorite subject.

   c) Physics has been studied for many centuries.

the Philippines,
the United Nations,
economics, politics

2. Use plural verbs after the following: any of, some of, all of, many, the rest of, a lot of, a number of, several.

   a) A number of my friends are from China.

   b) Many countries have joined the European Union.

   c) Several cars were damaged in the accident.

any of, some of, all of,
many, the rest of, a lot of,
a number of, several

3. Use either a singular or plural verb after the following nouns: jury, class, team, family, society. The meaning of the noun is dependent on the form of the verb used.

   a) The jury has made a decision.

   b) The class are ready for their exam.

jury, class, team, family,
society

Preposition

Usage

to sea
to the bathroom
to the front
to the reporter

To

a) He walked to school.

b) I work from nine to five.

c) We don't know the answer to this problem.

Grammar Exercises

Choose the correct word or phrase to complete each sentence.

Hint

1. Simon and I (am / are) going to the park this afternoon.

   Simon and I

2. Can you finish cleaning the house (until / by) seven o'clock?

   finish cleaning

3. Peter and Sally (have / has) red bicycles.

   Peter and Sally

4. The Philippines (are / is) made up of many islands.

   The Philippines

5. I ate some food (for / during) the party.

   ----

6. Three hundred dollars (is / are) a lot of money.

   Three hundred dollars, money

7. A number of students in the class (has / have) cell phones.

   A number of students

8. After school, I met my friends (at / to) the park.

   met, the park

9. I have (been / was) here for two hours.

   ----

10. Some of the fish (were / was) sick.

    Some of the fish

Part 1 Picture Description

Listen and choose the statement that best describes the picture.

1. (A) (B) (C) (D)

2. (A) (B) (C) (D)

3. (A) (B) (C) (D)

4.    (A)   (B)   (C)   (D)

5.   (A)   (B)   (C)   (D)

Listen and choose the correct answer.

1.   (A)   (B)   (C)
2.   (A)   (B)   (C)
3.   (A)   (B)   (C)
4.   (A)   (B)   (C)
5.   (A)   (B)   (C)

Listen and choose the correct answer.

1. What does the man want to do?

   (A) Use the computer   (B) Break the computer
   (C) Fix the computer   (D) Buy the computer

2. What can't the woman do?

   (A) Use a computer   (B) Save documents
   (C) Sell computers   (D) Find a computer

3. What does the woman have tomorrow?

   (A) A meeting   (B) A big project
   (C) A business lunch   (D) A presentation

4. Where are the man and woman?

   (A) In a library   (B) At the movies
   (C) At a train station   (D) At a travel agency

5. What does the man want?

   (A) A ticket to New York   (B) A more expensive ticket
   (C) A ticket to Los Angeles   (D) A train ticket

6. What is the problem?

   (A) The man is sick.
   (B) The ticket is too expensive.
   (C) There are no more tickets.
   (D) The man lost his ticket.

Listen and choose the best answer to each question.

1. What time will the flight now be leaving at?

    (A) At 6:00
    (B) At 7:00
    (C) At 7:15
    (D) At 7:50

2. At what gate do the passengers now have to leave from?

    (A) 23A
    (B) 32A
    (C) 22B
    (D) 22A

3. Where is the flight traveling?

    (A) From Ireland to Spain
    (B) From Spain to Iceland
    (C) From Iceland to Spain
    (D) From Spain to Ireland

4. Where is the bear?

    (A) To the people's left
    (B) To the people's right
    (C) Behind the people
    (D) Above the people

5. Which is closest to King's age?

    (A) Five years
    (B) Seven years
    (C) Ten years
    (D) Sixteen years

6. How many bears do they have at Funland?

    (A) Nine
    (B) Eleven
    (C) Seven
    (D) Ten

Choose the word or phrase that best completes the sentence.

1.   I have worked for my ------- for two years.

    (A) employee   (B) apply
    (C) employer   (D) work

2.   Where ------- you yesterday? I waited for thirty minutes!

    (A) was   (B) have
    (C) were   (D) is

3.   I hurt my leg ------- the soccer match.

    (A) by   (B) over
    (C) been   (D) during

4.   I got up this morning ------- seven o'clock.

    (A) on   (B) in
    (C) from   (D) at

5.   It's raining. Could you ------- me your umbrella?

    (A) borrow   (B) until
    (C) lend   (D) remind

6.   We like ------- at parties.

    (A) to dance   (B) to dancing
    (C) dance   (D) have dance

7.   The students, as well as the teacher, ------- happy about the test results.

    (A) was   (B) are
    (C) is   (D) has

8. During the day, they ------- time to finish the work.

    (A) doesn't have   (B) not have

    (C) didn't have   (D) don't

9. I ------- to the doctor because I was sick.

    (A) go   (B) walk

    (C) was   (D) went

10. ------- people are not happy with the class.

    (A) Most of   (B) Every

    (C) Many a   (D) A number of

11. I have to finish ------- seven o'clock.

    (A) during   (B) by

    (C) until   (D) on

12. All of the food ------- prepared by seven.

    (A) were   (B) has

    (C) have   (D) was

13. All of the people there ------- from Japan.

    (A) were   (B) is

    (C) be   (D) was

14. It took a lot of ------- to find the Titanic.

    (A) afford   (B) effort

    (C) strong   (D) fewer

15. I went to the city ------- train.

    (A) by   (B) for

    (C) before   (D) through

Choose the best word or phrase for each blank.

<u>Questions 1 through 3</u> refer to the following memo.

Memo

To: All employees
From: Jason Irving
Re: Free presentation

There will be a free **1.** ------- in the large conference room on January 15th. Gregory

        (A) present
        (B) presentation
        (C) representative
        (D) representation

Souza, from the personnel department, will be **2.** ------- about his new book. All

        (A) speech
        (B) telling
        (C) speaking
        (D) talk

employees are welcome to **3.** ------- . All participants will receive a complimentary

        (A) attend
        (B) attentive
        (C) attending
        (D) attendant

copy of his book, which deals with problems and solutions of working in a company.

Questions 4 through 6 refer to the following letter.

Woodworks
23 Culver Lane
Westford
12034

Alice Burns
934 Garden Highway
Fremont

Dear Ms. Burns,

Thank you for your recent enquiries about "Woodworks." Woodworks **4.** ------- a small

(A) are
(B) be
(C) is
(D) has

family-owned company. We are in our sixth year of business. We specialize in hand-carved pieces. We **5.** ------- local wood and make sure three trees are planted

(A) uses
(B) use
(C) used to
(D) using

to replace every tree we use. Woodworks has its own forest, and all of our products are made from trees that grow there. As you say, we are a little expensive. However, we make a unique, high-quality product. Every piece we make is designed individually. It takes about six months to make **6.** ------- of our products. Of course,

(A) every
(B) everyone
(C) each
(D) anyone

this costs a lot of money.
Please enjoy the enclosed catalog.
Sincerely,

Emma Richards

Choose the best answer.

Questions 1 and 2 refer to the following advertisement.

For Sale

Used car — Daewoo Nubira (five years old)
New CD player and tires. Color — green
Only $3000
Call Linda at (212) 917-7282 between 9 a.m. — 6 p.m.

For Sale

Nissan Primera (six years old)
Some damage. Needs new doors.
Color — black and purple
$1500
Call John at (214) 873-6582

1. What are these advertisements for?

   (A) To sell new cars
   (B) To sell old cars
   (C) To buy new cars
   (D) To buy old cars

2. How old is the Nissan?

   (A) Two years old
   (B) Three years old
   (C) Five years old
   (D) Six years old

Questions 3 through 5 refer to the following advertisement.

Do you want to learn to play the guitar? Now, you can do it in just one week! For only $35, you can get our new book with two CDs. Learn to play the guitar quickly in your own home.

If you are interested in lessons, we have classes at our school three times a week, from 7 p.m. – 9 p.m. Our two experienced teachers have been teaching the guitar for over ten years.

For more information, call Michael at 335-4287.

3. What do you get for $35?

(A) A book
(B) One teacher
(C) A book and two CDs
(D) A guitar

4. How long have their teachers been teaching for?

(A) Five years
(B) Two years
(C) Ten years
(D) Three years

5. How often does the school have guitar classes?

(A) Once a week
(B) Twice a week
(C) Two hours
(D) Three times a week

Questions 6 through 9 refer to the following letters.

Dear Jenny,
    It's been a long time since I last saw you. A lot has happened since then. I got a new job working at a toy company. It's more interesting than my old job at the post office. I also got a new apartment. It's nice and big. If you have time, you should come visit me soon. I have a vacation next month, so you could visit me then. Call me soon!

Love,
Sarah

Dear Sarah,
    It was great to get your letter. My classes are going well, and I got an A in every subject this semester. The winter vacation starts next month. I have to find a part-time job, so I won't have much free time. Maybe I will have more time during the summer vacation to visit you. I'll call you next week.
Take care,

Jenny

6. Where does Sarah work now?

(A) At a restaurant   (B) In an apartment
(C) At a toy company   (D) At the post office

7. When does Sarah have a vacation?

(A) In one week   (B) In one month
(C) In three months   (D) Next year

8. What does Sarah ask Jenny to do?

(A) Call her   (B) Work at the post office
(C) Go to the toy company   (D) Get a new apartment

9. Which of the following is probably NOT true?

(A) Jenny will visit Sarah next month.
(B) Jenny is a student.
(C) Jenny and Sarah are friends.
(D) Sarah likes her new job.

Auxiliaries

Vocabulary

A. LISTENING (Communication I)

Listen and write the letter of the statement that best describes the picture.

Exercise 1

1. _____   2. _____   3. _____   4. _____

Exercise 2

1. _____   2. _____   3. _____   4. _____

B. READING (Commonly Confused Words)

Choose the correct word to complete each sentence.

Exercise 1

1. It's raining. (Bring / Take) an umbrella when you leave.
2. Please (bring / take) your sister when you come to my party.

Exercise 2

1. What (advice / advise) can you give me?
2. I'd (advice / advise) you to save some money.

Exercise 3

1. She (said / told) hello to him.
2. He (said / told) her to be quiet.

Exercise 1
1. (B) Say   2. (A) Call
3. (D) Chat   4. (C) Shout

Exercise 2
1. (B) Talk   2. (D) Yell
3. (A) Speak 4. (C) Whisper

Exercise 1
1. take   2. bring

Exercise 2
1. advice 2. advise

Exercise 3
1. said   2. told

Auxiliaries

1. Auxiliaries

   a) I should do my homework now.

   b) I can help you clean the car.

2. Semi-auxiliaries

   I am able to dance very well.

3. Differences between auxiliaries and other verbs

   ▶ **Auxiliary verbs are followed by the basic form of a verb.**

   You must (clean / ~~to clean~~ / ~~cleans~~) your room now.

   ▶ **Auxiliary verbs are NOT used with to-infinitives.**

   I would like to (be able to / ~~can~~) speak English.

   ▶ **Auxiliary verbs do not agree with the subject in number.**

   John (can / ~~cans~~) swim very well.

   ▶ **To negate an auxiliary verb, add "not" after it.**

   I (will not / ~~don't will~~) attend the meeting.

   ▶ **It is possible to delete verb phrases after an auxiliary when they are repeated.**

   a) John will come to the party and so will Marta.
   b) George can play the guitar, but Larry can't.
   c) "I like apples." "So do I."

4. Making negative and interrogative sentences

Auxiliaries	Negative sentences	Interrogative sentences
can	cannot	Can you ~?
ought to	ought not to	Ought you to ~?
had better	had better not	—
have to	do not have to	Do you have to ~?
be going to	be not going to	Are you going to ~?
used to	did not use to	Did you use to ~?
would rather	would rather not	Would you rather ~?

5. Use *would* and *could* instead of *will* and *can* for proposals.

   (Would / ~~Will~~) you like to have some coffee?

By

a) I went to school by subway.
b) You have to finish it by next week.
c) We can improve our English by practicing.

Sidebar (Grammar Focus):

can, could, may, might,
will, would, shall, should,
must . . .

ought to, have to,
be able to . . .

Sidebar (Preposition):

Usage

by bus
by tomorrow
by practicing
by someone
by the door

Grammar Exercises

Choose the correct word or phrase to complete each sentence.

Hint

1. I could (clean / cleaned) the room for you.

   could

2. David practices English every day to (can / be able to) speak it fluently.

   to

3. Linda (can / cans) skate really well.

   skate

4. We (ought to not / ought not to) eat too much.

   ----

5. You'd better (taking a / take a) good rest after hiking.

   You'd better

6. (Will / Would) you care for something to drink?

   care

7. You had (not better / better not) keep the plants outside during winter.

   had better

8. Karen can play the flute really well and (so can / so does) Lars.

   can play

9. We (will not / don't will) go to the meeting tomorrow morning.

   ----

10. They (don't have to / have not to) submit the report by Friday.

Part 1 Picture Description

Listen and choose the statement that best describes the picture.

1.

    (A)   (B)   (C)   (D)

2.   (A)   (B)   (C)   (D)

3.

    (A)   (B)   (C)   (D)

4.    (A)   (B)   (C)   (D)

5.   (A)   (B)   (C)   (D)

Part 2 Questions and Responses

Listen and choose the correct answer.

1.   (A)   (B)   (C)
2.   (A)   (B)   (C)
3.   (A)   (B)   (C)
4.   (A)   (B)   (C)
5.   (A)   (B)   (C)

Listen and choose the correct answer.

1. Where does the woman want to go?

    (A) To the library   (B) To the post office
    (C) To the bookstore   (D) Next door

2. How long will it take to walk there?

    (A) No more than ten minutes
    (B) Fifteen minutes
    (C) One hour
    (D) At least ten minutes

3. When does the woman need to be in the city center?

    (A) In half an hour   (B) In sixty minutes
    (C) In two hours   (D) In forty minutes

4. Where is the man going?

    (A) To work   (B) To school
    (C) To the store   (D) To a funeral

5. What does the woman want?

    (A) Chinese food   (B) A book
    (C) Some eggs   (D) Some milk

6. How many kinds of items will the man bring home?

    (A) One   (B) Two
    (C) Three   (D) Four

Listen and choose the best answer to each question.

1. Why does the man like his job?

    (A) It is very easy.
    (B) He works short hours.
    (C) He likes his co-worker.
    (D) It doesn't feel like a job to him.

2. What kind of place does the person want to sing in?

    (A) In a bar   (B) In a restaurant
    (C) In the theater   (D) In the park

3. Who does the man sing with?

    (A) His cousin   (B) His father
    (C) His brother   (D) His friend

4. Who is this ad aimed at?

    (A) People with new cell phones   (B) People with old computers
    (C) People with old cell phones   (D) People with new computers

5. When will this sale take place?

    (A) On Monday   (B) On Wednesday
    (C) On Thursday   (D) On the weekend

6. What would you be if you missed this sale?

    (A) Angry   (B) Sad
    (C) Sleepy   (D) Crazy

Choose the word or phrase that best completes the sentence.

1. The game ------- finish in two hours.

    (A) will   (B) want
    (C) ought   (D) have to

2. I'd better ------- to bed now to get up early in the morning.
    (A) go   (B) going
    (C) to go   (D) went

3. If you are sick, you ------- go to school.

    (A) should not   (B) may
    (C) would   (D) ought to not

4. The airplane ------- at 3:30 p.m.

    (A) arrive   (B) arriving
    (C) is arrive   (D) arrives

5. Could you ------- me my red sweater, please?

    (A) take   (B) advise
    (C) borrow   (D) bring

6. You ------- cross the road yet.

    (A) ought not to   (B) not ought to
    (C) ought to not   (D) don't ought to

7. We would ------- out. It's freezing outside.

    (A) not rather go   (B) rather not go
    (C) not rather to go   (D) rather not to go

8. We have ------- solved the problem.

    (A) already   (B) could

    (C) yet   (D) can

9. This time next year, she will ------- play the piano very well.

    (A) can   (B) should

    (C) be able to   (D) ought to

10. Every morning, I meet my friend ------- the way to school.

    (A) on   (B) to

    (C) from   (D) in

11. ------- you like coffee or tea?

    (A) Would   (B) Could

    (C) Should   (D) Will

12. Would you like ------- with me?

    (A) to go shopping   (B) to shopping

    (C) shopping to   (D) shop to go

13. What did she ------- you to do?

    (A) say   (B) speak

    (C) advice   (D) tell

14. We will get there ------- a few minutes.

    (A) in   (B) on

    (C) at   (D) by

15. Tomorrow morning, you have to be up ------- six o'clock.

    (A) on   (B) by

    (C) in   (D) to

Choose the best word or phrase for each blank.

Questions 1 through 3 refer to the following email.

To: jlopez@cbt.com
From: rmartin@cbt.com
Subject: Pep talk

Hi Jenny,

This is a quick email to **1.** ------- you that I know you are having a hard time. We are

        (A) tell
        (B) speak
        (C) say
        (D) talk

all here to help you, so come talk to anyone whenever you want. If you have time this week, how about meeting after work? I'd like to buy you a coffee and we **2.** ------- have a chat. Please let me know if you think this is a good idea or not. Could

    (A) had
    (B) could
    (C) advice
    (D) would

you give me your reply **3.** ------- four o'clock today?

        (A) on
        (B) within
        (C) before
        (D) along

Cheers,
Rachel

Questions 4 through 6 refer to the following complaint form.

Pentagon's Restaurants
Customer Comments Form
Date of visit: Jan 31st
Time of visit: 11 a.m.
Branch name: Rochester High Street

Comments
This is the first **4.** ------- I have eaten at Pentagon's. However, I think it will also be

    (A) time
    (B) event
    (C) turn
    (D) eating

the last. I had to wait thirty minutes for my food. I had to ask the waitress four times before she brought water to our table. I **5.** ------- not enjoy a conversation with

    (A) had
    (B) was
    (C) do
    (D) could

my friend because of the noise from the kitchen. The staff **6.** ------- shouting and

    (A) ought not
    (B) had to
    (C) were
    (D) did

yelling at each other the whole time. I asked to speak to the manager, but he was not available. The food was very good, but not good enough to make me want to return to any of your restaurants.

Choose the best answer.

<u>Questions 1 and 2</u> refer to the following advertisement.

Special Sale
At Bathland!
Everything that you need for your bathroom
For two weeks only!
50% off our extra-large luxury bathtubs
30% off luxury soap and shampoo sets
Buy two large towels and get one free
Mirrors, sinks, shelves, tiles, and much more . . .
All up to 25% off!

1. What would you NOT buy at Bathland?

   (A) A television   (B) Towels
   (C) Soap   (D) A mirror

2. How long will the sale last?

   (A) For ten days   (B) For one month
   (C) Forever   (D) For fourteen days

Questions 3 through 5 refer to the following letter.

Dear Jane,

How are you? I'm at my aunt and uncle's house in the country. I'm having a great time. The country air is so clean. I ride horses every day with my uncle. He is giving me lots of advice. My aunt cooks delicious food for every meal. She taught me how to make chocolate chip cookies. I would like to stay for another week, but I can't. My vacation will be over. I will see you in two days, and I will tell you all about it.

Your friend,
Susan

3. Where do Susan's aunt and uncle live?

(A) In the city   (B) In the country
(C) At the beach   (D) In an apartment

4. What does Susan do there?

(A) Feed animals   (B) Work in the garden
(C) Swim in the lake   (D) Ride horses

5. What did Susan's aunt teach her?

(A) How to make cookies   (B) How to ride a horse
(C) How to write a letter   (D) How to live in the country

Questions 6 through 9 refer to the following table and email.

Asia Pacific Weather: Five-Day Forecast January 7th-11th

Beijing	-4°C,	cloudy, with some snow
Tokyo	0°C,	sunny, with some clouds in the evening
Hong Kong	14°C,	cloudy, with sunshine in the morning
Seoul	3°C,	sunny, some light rain in the afternoon
Singapore	27°C,	windy and rainy, with some lightning
Jakarta	26°C,	heavy rain, some lightning at night
Sydney	19°C,	windy and cloudy all day

To: Alice Souza <aasouza@netmail.co>
From: MJames@mailhouse.com
Subject: Forecast
Date: January 7th

Dear Ms. Souza,

Here is the weather forecast that you asked for. Your trip starts in Beijing. It will be very cold there, so bring lots of warm clothes. On January 10th, you will go to Singapore. It will be hot, so you need light clothes. I think you should also pack an umbrella.
Have a good trip, and don't hesitate to call me if you have any questions.

Sincerely,
Marilyn James

6. Which city has the highest temperature?

(A) Beijing   (B) Seoul
(C) Singapore   (D) Sydney

7. Which city has the lowest temperature?

(A) Beijing   (B) Seoul
(C) Singapore   (D) Sydney

8. Which city will have the most rain?

(A) Hong Kong   (B) Tokyo
(C) Jakarta   (D) Singapore

9. Why did Alice Souza want to know the weather forecast?

(A) Because it is her hobby
(B) Because she is taking a trip
(C) Because she wants to buy new clothes
(D) Because she doesn't like rain

Relative Pronouns

V o c a b u l a r y

A. LISTENING (Communication II)

Listen and write the letter of the statement that best describes the picture.

Exercise 1

1. _____ 2. _____ 3. _____ 4. _____

Exercise 1
1. (B) Point   2. (A) Raise
3. (D) Write   4. (C) Wave

Exercise 2

1. _____ 2. _____ 3. _____ 4. _____

Exercise 2
1. (A) Hug   2. (B) Help
3. (D) Cheer   4. (C) Show

B. READING (Commonly Confused Words)

Choose the correct word to complete each sentence.

Exercise 1

1. That book had a strong (affect / effect) on how I think.
2. The weather can (affect / effect) the way you feel.

Exercise 1
1. effect   2. affect

Exercise 2

1. Would you like (another / other) glass of beer?
2. I prefer the (another / other) book to this one.

Exercise 2
1. another   2. other

Exercise 3

1. He was cooking (when / while) she arrived home.
2. He was playing tennis (when / while) she was shopping.

Exercise 3
1. when   2. while

Relative Pronouns

1. Subjective case of relative pronouns

▶ **When the antecedent is a person, use *who, that,* or *whoever*.**

a) That's the boy who came to our party last week.
b) They are giving a free mug to whoever comes to the store today.

▶ **When the antecedent is an animal or object, use *which* or *that*.**

a) The dog, which took my shoes, belongs to Amy.
b) The pen that he wrote his novel with is in the museum.
c) The dog which took my shoes belongs to Amy. (X)
d) The pen, that he wrote his novel with, is in the museum. (X)

> **Note** The number of the verb in a relative clause is decided by its antecedent.

a) I saw a boy who was running in the park.
b) Don likes some of the fish that are in the tank.

2. Possessive case of relative pronouns

▶ **When the antecedent is a person, animal, or object, use *whose*.**

a) I know the man whose car was stolen.
b) Maria was walking a dog whose ears were very long.

3. Objective case of relative pronouns

▶ **When the antecedent is a person, use *who(m)*.**

a) She is the girl (who) I met in the park.
b) She is the girl to whom I gave a free ticket.

▶ **When the antecedent is an animal or an object, use *which* or *that*.**

a) The hamster (that) I keep in my room is two years old now.

4. It is ~ that/who

a) It was my father who helped me with my homework yesterday.
b) It was yesterday that my father helped me with my homework.

5. Preposition + relative pronoun

a) This is the house in which I have lived for ten years.
b) That was the day on which I met her for the first time.
c) That is the reason for which I was late for the appointment.
d) This is the house in that I have lived for ten years. (X)

> **Note** The relative pronoun "that" is not used with prepositions.

Preposition

With

with a pen
with a friend
with pleasure
with me

a) She cut the banana with a knife.
b) I went shopping with my mother.
c) He doesn't have any money with him.

Choose the correct word or phrase to complete each sentence.

1. I know the woman (who / which) is sitting over there.

2. The car (whose / that) is parked near the tree belongs to my friend.

3. Adam bought his son a bicycle (that / whose) color is red and blue.

4. Could we have that meeting (other / another) time?

5. It's next week (which / that) we have to finish the project.

6. The girl (who / whom) called didn't leave her name.

7. This is the book (in that / in which) I read about Chinese culture.

8. July 4th is the date (on which / in which) the United States became independent.

9. The hotel (where / when) we stayed didn't have a restaurant.

10. That's the reason (where / why) he couldn't come to the meeting.

Part 1 Picture Description

Listen and choose the statement that best describes the picture.

1.   (A)   (B)   (C)   (D)

2.   (A)   (B)   (C)   (D)

3.   (A)   (B)   (C)   (D)

4.  (A) (B) (C) (D)

5.   (A) (B) (C) (D)

Part 2 Questions and Responses

Listen and choose the correct answer.

1. (A)   (B)   (C)

2. (A)   (B)   (C)

3. (A)   (B)   (C)

4. (A)   (B)   (C)

5. (A)   (B)   (C)

Listen and choose the correct answer.

1. Where is this conversation taking place?

   (A) On the telephone   (B) On the radio
   (C) On the television   (D) In a store

2. What does the man want to know?

   (A) The woman's phone number
   (B) How to find the bookstore
   (C) When the store is open
   (D) The price of a book

3. What time does the store open on Saturdays?

   (A) Ten o'clock   (B) Nine o'clock
   (C) Five o'clock   (D) Six o'clock

4. What color are the gloves the man is searching for?

   (A) Red   (B) Brown
   (C) Blue and brown   (D) Blue

5. Who gave the gloves to the man?

   (A) His wife   (B) The woman
   (C) His mother   (D) His sister

6. What does the woman say about the gloves?

   (A) She wants a pair like them.
   (B) She has a pair like them.
   (C) They are on the chair.
   (D) She doesn't know where they are.

Listen and choose the best answer to each question.

1. How did the speaker feel when she first went to America?

   (A) Lonely   (B) Happy
   (C) Sad   (D) Hungry

2. Which of these did the speaker NOT mention about first being in America?

   (A) She didn't like the food.   (B) She had no friends.
   (C) She didn't like the weather.   (D) She didn't have any fun places to go to.

3. Why does the speaker like America now?

   (A) She likes the weather and the food.
   (B) She has lots of friends and likes the weather.
   (C) She has lots of friends and things to do.
   (D) She likes the weather and has lots of things to do.

4. When did the speaker start taking Taekwondo lessons?

   (A) Last month   (B) Two years ago
   (C) Last year   (D) Last Christmas

5. How does the speaker feel after doing Taekwondo for so long?

   (A) Faster and angrier   (B) Stronger and lighter
   (C) Lighter and angrier   (D) Faster and stronger

6. What does the speaker want to get next year?

   (A) A red belt   (B) A blue belt
   (C) A brown belt   (D) None of the above

Choose the word or phrase that best completes the sentence.

1. Soccer is the sport ------- I like the most.

   (A) who   (B) that
   (C) whom   (D) whose

2. The hotel ------- we stayed was built 100 years ago.

   (A) when   (B) which
   (C) that   (D) where

3. The man ------- Linda spoke was her English teacher.

   (A) who   (B) whose
   (C) to whom   (D) that

4. Could you give me ------- pen, please?

   (A) whose   (B) other
   (C) whom   (D) another

5. I didn't ------- whose car it was.

   (A) saw   (B) see
   (C) look   (D) speak

6. Jane is the girl ------- mother wrote a famous novel.

   (A) whose   (B) who
   (C) that   (D) which

7. This is the course in ------- we learned the history of England.

   (A) that   (B) which
   (C) where   (D) whose

8. The trip to India was a lot of -------.

(A) funny

(B) fun

(C) already

(D) yet

9. The greatest writer ------- I have ever met was Neil Smith.

(A) whose

(B) that

(C) which

(D) where

10. What ------- did that movie have on her?

(A) advise

(B) affect

(C) effect

(D) advice

11. December 31st is the date ------- we meet every year.

(A) in which

(B) by which

(C) on which

(D) where

12. Please ------- me to go to the bank.

(A) remind

(B) while

(C) when

(D) mind

13. The book was written ------- Lisa Smith.

(A) at

(B) by

(C) of

(D) in

14. They have ------- in Canada for two years.

(A) is

(B) be

(C) were

(D) been

15. I spoke ------- my teacher after the exam.

(A) on

(B) by

(C) with

(D) at

Choose the best word or phrase for each blank.

<u>Questions 1 through 3</u> refer to the following notice.

Notice

From next week, all cars **1.** ------- are parked in front of the building will be towed

        (A) who
        (B) whose
        (C) that
        (D) what

away. Any employees who want to park near the building must apply for a special permit. All cars **2.** ------- a permit sticker will be allowed to park in the car park

        (A) by
        (B) for
        (C) in
        (D) with

surrounding the building. Drivers who want a permit must visit the personnel office and fill in a form. You will have to pay $5 to receive your sticker when you fill in the form. Please call 843-9876 for **3.** ------- information.

        (A) more
        (B) add
        (C) plus
        (D) over

Questions 4 through 6 refer to the following letter.

Rirakku Designs
Ikaruga City
221900
Tel: 81-(0)73-998-743

Dear Ms. Hives,

I am **4.** ------- you the designs that you asked for. I hope that you like them. If you

      (A) send
      (B) sent
      (C) sending
      (D) to send

are not happy with the work that I have done, please call me. My telephone number is **5.** ------- the top of this page. I tried to include all the colors that you

      (A) at
      (B) by
      (C) with
      (D) in

wanted. I have been in hospital. That is the reason **6.** ------- I have sent this a little

      (A) for
      (B) which
      (C) why
      (D) when

later than you expected. I am sorry for the inconvenience. Please let me know the exact date that you need the finished product.

Thank you for using Rirakku Designs.

Sincerely,
Ken Miyoshi

Choose the best answer.

Questions 1 and 2 refer to the following note.

Dear Michael,

I am going shopping for the day. I have to buy a new table and chairs. I won't be home until eight o'clock this evening. Please take the dog for a walk and don't forget to clean your room. Your dinner is in the microwave. There is some orange juice in the refrigerator, too. See you later!

-Mom

1. Who wrote the note?

   (A) Michael   (B) Michael's mother
   (C) Michael's teacher (D) Michael's sister

2. What should Michael do?

   (A) Wash the dishes   (B) Feed the dog
   (C) Clean his room   (D) Clean the dog

Questions 3 through 5 refer to the following article.

We asked 100 students, "What is your favorite class?" Here are their answers:

- Math - 15
- Science - 35
- English - 20
- Music - 30

We also asked the reasons why these students preferred the class. These are the most popular answers:

1) They liked the teacher.
2) The class was easy.
3) They had good friends in the class.

We then asked the students, "What is your least favorite class?" Here are their answers:

- Math - 25
- Physical education - 45
- History - 15
- Geography - 15

3. What is the most popular class?

(A) Math   (B) Science
(C) English   (D) Music

4. Why might students like their class?

(A) Their teacher is angry.   (B) The class is boring.
(C) They don't like the class.   (D) They like their teacher.

5. Which of these classes is most disliked by students?

(A) Science   (B) Physical education
(C) Music   (D) English

Questions 6 through 9 refer to the following memo and sign.

To: All life guards
From: Beachside City Council
Re: Beach rules and competition

The summer season is nearly here, so we would like to remind you about the beach rules. We will put this sign up at every beach. All life guards must keep a copy of the rules in their life-saving kit. Also, we will have a volleyball competition every day this summer. Please do not watch the competition. Keep your eyes on the sea.
Have a great summer!

CITY BEACH

Open: May 31st — August 31st

10:00 a.m. — 9:00 p.m.
- Special volleyball competition between 2:00 and 5:00
- First prize — $200
- All entrants must be over sixteen years old.
- Each team must have two players.
- Each team must have one male and one female.

BEACH RULES
No animals.
No camping.
No glass bottles.
No cars or motorcycles.
Children under eight years must be with an adult.

6. When is the beach NOT open?

(A) June 4th
(B) April 5th
(C) July 30th
(D) August 1st

7. Who shouldn't go alone to the beach?

(A) Adults
(B) Teenagers
(C) Children over ten years
(D) Children under eight years

8. Which team would be allowed to play in the competition?

(A) Two men
(B) Two women
(C) A man and a woman
(D) A man and a fifteen-year-old girl

9. Which of the following is NOT true?

(A) Lifeguards should watch the volleyball competition.
(B) The beach is open for three months.
(C) Cars cannot drive on the beach.
(D) You cannot take glass bottles onto the beach.

Vocabulary

A. LISTENING (Food)

Listen and write the letter of the statement that best describes the picture.

Exercise 1

1. _____

2. _____

3. _____

4. _____

Exercise 1
1. (D) Feed   2. (C) Chew
3. (B) Have   4. (A) Eat

Exercise 2

1. _____

2. _____

3. _____

4. _____

Exercise 2
1. (B) Pour   2. (A) Cook
3. (D) Bring   4. (C) Give

B. READING (Commonly Confused Words)

Choose the correct word to complete each sentence.

Exercise 1

1. The (desert / dessert) is hot and dry.
2. The (desert / dessert) was delicious!

Exercise 1
1. desert   2. dessert

Exercise 2

1. He ate (a little / a few) of his birthday cake.
2. He ate (a little / a few) cookies.

Exercise 2
1. a little   2. a few

Exercise 3

1. I want (any / some) ice cream.
2. We don't have (any / some) ice cream.

Exercise 3
1. some   2. any

Grammar Focus

Nouns / Pronouns

1. Countable nouns (common nouns, collective nouns) use *a/an* for singular forms and add *s/es* for plural forms.
   a) We have an orange cat.
   b) Look at the cars on the street.
   c) Do you have a sweater I could borrow?

2. Uncountable nouns (material nouns, proper nouns, abstract nouns) cannot be used with *a/an* or as a plural form.
   a) The horse needs food and water.
   b) I need ten sheets of paper.

3. The following are uncountable nouns: furniture, luggage, baggage, news, information, mail.
   a) We bought a lot of furniture for our new house.
   b) How many pieces of baggage do you have?

4. Nouns can act as subjects, complements, and objects.
   a) *Michael* works for a computer company.
   b) Lucy is *a travel agent*.
   c) Everyone is looking for *the lost child*.

5. Personal pronouns

		subjective	possessive	objective	possessive pronoun	reflexive pronoun
1st person	singular	I	my	me	mine	myself
	plural	we	our	us	ours	ourselves
2nd person	singular	you	your	you	yours	yourself
	plural	you	your	you	yours	yourselves
3rd person	singular	he	his	him	his	himself
	singular	she	her	her	hers	herself
	singular	it	its	it		itself
	singular	they	their	them	theirs	themselves

6. Indefinite pronouns
   a) I have two pens; *one* is blue and *the other* is black.
   b) There are ten boys; *some* are in the room, and *the others* are in the yard.

Preposition

For

a) I went to the bakery for some bread.
b) They have lived here for five years.
c) We bought a phone for $100.

Usage

for six weeks
for fifty dollars
for some candy
for work

Choose the correct word or phrase to complete each sentence.

Hint

1. Where are you going to put all your (furniture / furnitures)?

   ----

2. There are no (battery / batteries) in the radio.

   are

3. Bad news (don't / doesn't) make people happy.

   news

4. We had a lot of (luggage / luggages).

   ----

5. What (kind / kinds) of camera do you have?

   camera

6. Three years (is / are) a long time to be without a job.

   Three years

7. I was waiting for her at the (reception / receptions) desk.

   desk

8. A large number of (person / people) in this country are immigrants.

   a number of

9. Karen has (few / little) friends at the company.

   friends

10. Did you get the (mails / mail) yet?

Part 1 Picture Description

Listen and choose the statement that best describes the picture.

1.   (A)   (B)   (C)   (D)

2.   (A)   (B)   (C)   (D)

3.   (A)   (B)   (C)   (D)

4.  (A) (B) (C) (D)

5.   (A) (B) (C) (D)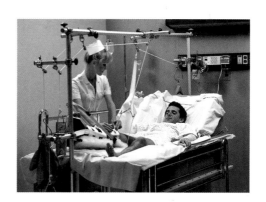

Part 2 Questions and Responses

Listen and choose the correct answer.

1. (A) (B) (C)
2. (A) (B) (C)
3. (A) (B) (C)
4. (A) (B) (C)
5. (A) (B) (C)

Listen and choose the correct answer.

1. Who is Mary?

   (A) The new accountant   (B) The old accountant
   (C) A new teacher   (D) The manager

2. What is Mary wearing?

   (A) A black dress and a red jacket
   (B) Red pants
   (C) A black suit
   (D) A red dress and a black jacket

3. Why is the man surprised?

   (A) He thought Mary was taller.
   (B) He expected Mary to talk to him.
   (C) He thought Mary would look older.
   (D) Mary is his old school friend.

4. What are the man and woman talking about?

   (A) Making cookies   (B) Going on a picnic
   (C) Opening a restaurant   (D) Going on vacation

5. What does the woman want to know?

   (A) If she needs to bring anything
   (B) If she should pay a fee
   (C) If the man can give her a ride
   (D) What time she should arrive

6. When will the man and woman next meet?

   (A) The following morning   (B) Tomorrow night
   (C) Next week   (D) At 11 p.m.

Listen and choose the best answer to each question.

1. What does Pablo enjoy about Korea?

   (A) The universities   (B) The food
   (C) The economy   (D) The cities

2. What is Pablo studying?

   (A) Spanish and business   (B) Korean and cooking
   (C) Spanish and Korea   (D) Economics and Korean

3. Where is he going next and when?

   (A) Madrid, next January   (B) Barcelona, next January
   (C) Barcelona, next February (D) Madrid, next February

---

4. What is the problem?

   (A) A car has a flat tire.
   (B) A car has been stolen.
   (C) A car has broken down.
   (D) A car is blocking the entrance.

5. What is the registration number of the car?

   (A) ST 4572   (B) ST 4571
   (C) SP 4571   (D) SP 5571

6. What should the owner of the car do?

   (A) Change the tire   (B) Go to the parking lot
   (C) Call the police   (D) Buy a new car

Choose the word or phrase that best completes the sentence.

1. Did you buy ------- I asked you for?

   (A) a toothpaste   (B) a toothpastes
   (C) the toothpastes   (D) the toothpaste

2. Have you seen ------- stapler?

   (A) I'm   (B) my
   (C) mine   (D) me

3. Do you have ------- rooms available?

   (A) some   (B) sometime
   (C) sometimes   (D) any

4. I can do my homework by -------.

   (A) mine   (B) me
   (C) myself   (D) my

5. I don't have ------- money left.

   (A) much   (B) another
   (C) many   (D) a few

6. I was cooking ------- I burnt my finger.

   (A) while   (B) when
   (C) during   (D) by

7. I cut ten -------.

   (A) slice of bread   (B) slices of bread
   (C) slices of breads   (D) slice of breads

8. I worked for ------- hours on Sunday.

    (A) a little   (B) less

    (C) a few   (D) any

9. After you collect the money, you need to count -------.

    (A) it   (B) them

    (C) they   (D) anything

10. I ------- the bus there yesterday.

    (A) take   (B) bring

    (C) took   (D) went

11. There are two balls in the box. One is white and ------- is blue and red.

    (A) other   (B) others

    (C) the other   (D) the others

12. ------- you pour me some tea, please?

    (A) Can   (B) Mind

    (C) Ought   (D) Rather you to

13. I met a lot of ------- at the party.

    (A) peoples   (B) people

    (C) person   (D) persons

14. ------- is good for you.

    (A) Jogging   (B) Jogs

    (C) To jogging   (D) Jog

15. Please fill the glass ------- cold water.

    (A) for   (B) with

    (C) of   (D) to

Choose the best word or phrase for each blank.

Questions 1 through 3 refer to the following email.

To: Everyone
From: cc021@exxnet.co
Subject: Party
Date: October 20th

Hi Everyone,

As you know, the office halloween party is coming up. As usual, we will have a costume competition. It is a **1.** ------- for you all to have some fun and win some great

(A) chance
(B) change
(C) concept
(D) challenge

prizes. The party starts at 6 p.m. on Friday, October 30th. We will be closing the office early, so you will have one hour to get **2.** ------- . I am looking forward to some

(A) rest
(B) real
(C) ready
(D) realize

great costumes. This year, the first prize is free membership at the company sports club for one year. Second prize is dinner **3.** ------- the Magic Chef restaurant for four

(A) in
(B) at
(C) with
(D) for

people. See you on the 30th.

Miranda Kim

Questions 4 through 6 refer to the following memo.

Memo

To: All employees
From: Staff catering
Re: Staff cafeteria
Date: August 24th

We regret to inform you that we have to close **4.** ------- new staff cafeteria. We do not

(A) our
(B) their
(C) ours
(D) mine

know when we can **5.** ------- it again. Yesterday, twenty people became very sick after

(A) close
(B) open
(C) redo
(D) shut

eating their lunch at the cafeteria. They have severe food poisoning. Most of them are now OK, but some of them are still in the hospital. This is terrible news, so to protect your health, we have **6.** ------- to close the cafeteria. The sandwich store in the

(A) decided
(B) decision
(C) defence
(D) determination

basement will stay open. There have not been any problems with their food products. We apologize for the inconvenience and hope you all stay healthy.

Choose the best answer.

Questions 1 and 2 refer to the following poster.

Lost Puppy

Please help us find our puppy. She has been missing for two days. Her name is Potato Chip. She is small and white with brown spots. She is about six months old. She was last seen running through the park on Elm Street. She is very friendly and will come to you if you call her name. If you find her, please call us at 555-9837. A small reward is available.

1. What does the missing puppy look like?

    (A) She has white spots.   (B) She has brown spots.
    (C) She is small and yellow.   (D) She is big and black.

2. When should you call the telephone number?

    (A) If you eat potato chips   (B) If you are friendly
    (C) If your puppy is lost   (D) If you find Potato Chip

Questions 3 through 5 refer to the following notice.

ANNOUNCEMENT: TIME CHANGE

Tuesday's Movie Club meeting at the Megaplex cinema will be moved to Friday at 3:00 p.m. We will be watching the movie *The Wizard of Oz.* It is the 20th time we have shown it. During the movie, we will serve popcorn and drinks at our usual low prices. Remember, as part of our special offer, this week you can bring one friend for free. We have seating for only 300 people. This is one of our most popular movies, so don't be late. We hope to see you soon.

3. Which of the following is true?

(A) The meeting will be on Tuesday.
(B) The meeting will be moved from Friday to Tuesday.
(C) The meeting will be on Friday.
(D) The meeting will be moved from Thursday to Friday.

4. What is the special offer?

(A) Free popcorn　　　　　(B) Free drinks
(C) A free hotdog　　　　　(D) A free ticket for a friend

5. How many people can watch the movie?

(A) Three　　　　　(B) Twenty
(C) 300　　　　　(D) Everyone

Questions 6 through 9 refer to the following letter and catalog.

Dear Mrs. Smith,

To thank you for being one of our regular customers, I am pleased to let you know about a great new offer. We are having our end of summer sale. You can find great savings on our catalog prices for T-shirts. We have cut the prices for men's, women's, AND children's T-shirts. Your whole family can dress well and look good, but you don't have to spend a lot of money.

Please take a look at the attached catalog.

Regards,
Home and All Ltd.

Men's T-shirt
- 100% cotton   • Colors — white, green, blue
- Sizes — small, medium, large, X-large
  • **Price - $9.95**
- Buy 2, get one free

Women's T-shirt
- 100% cotton   • Colors — white, red, yellow, blue
- Sizes — small, medium, large
  • **Price - $8.95**
- Buy 1, get a free pair of socks

Children's T-shirt
- 100% cotton   • Colors — red, yellow, blue
- Sizes — small, medium, large
  • **Price - $6.95**

6. In which colors are men's T-shirts available?

   (A) White, red, blue   (B) White, green, yellow
   (C) White, green, blue   (D) Red, blue, yellow

7. How many men's T-shirts can you get for $40?

   (A) Three   (B) Four
   (C) Five   (D) Six

8. Mr. Smith, Mrs. Smith, and their son all want to buy T-shirts of the same color. What color can they get?

   (A) White   (B) Green
   (C) Yellow   (D) Blue

9. Why did Home and All send Mrs. Smith a catalog?

   (A) Because she asked for one
   (B) Because she is a regular customer
   (C) Because they have a lot of catalogs
   (D) Because they are friends

Adjectives / Adverbs

Vocabulary

A. LISTENING (Active Situations)

Listen and write the letter of the statement that best describes the picture.

Exercise 1

1. _____ 2. _____ 3. _____ 4. _____

Exercise 1
1. (B) Hop   3. (D) Chase
2. (C) Jump   4. (A) Load

Exercise 2

1. _____ 2. _____ 3. _____ 4. _____

Exercise 2
1. (C) Play   3. (D) March
2. (A) Fix   4. (B) Fly

B. READING (Commonly Confused Words)

Choose the correct word to complete each sentence.

Exercise 1

1. (Almost / Most) all of the children wanted to play soccer.
2. (Almost / Most) of the children wanted to play soccer.

Exercise 1
1. Almost   2. Most

Exercise 2

1. He worked (hard / hardly) all day. Now he is tired.
2. He (hard / hardly) worked today. He mostly relaxed.

Exercise 2
1. hard   2. hardly

Exercise 3

1. (Late / Lately), I have started jogging at night.
2. Did you come home (late / lately) last night?

Exercise 3
1. Lately   2. late

Adjectives / Adverbs

1. Adjectives

glad, sad, disgusted

▶ **adj + that**

a) I'm glad that you came.

b) It's important that we work together.

▶ **adj + to**

a) We are happy to be here.

b) I was shocked to see him.

bad at, bored of, interested in

▶ **adj + prep + ing**

a) She is good at playing tennis.

b) I'm tired of listening to this music.

▶ **Superlative form + to**

a) She was the last to arrive.

b) He's the oldest athlete to win a gold medal.

2. Adverbs

high / highly, near / nearly, free / freely

▶ **Adverbs can modify verbs, adjectives, other adverbs and clauses.**

a) She speaks English fluently and correctly.

b) You are entirely wrong.

c) He worked really hard.

d) I nearly fell over his feet.

always, usually, frequently, generally, often, occasionally, sometimes, hardly ever, seldom, never, rarely

▶ **Adverbs of frequency come after an auxiliary verb and before a main verb.**

a) She can rarely drive to work in less that an hour.

b) You should always brush your teeth after eating.

Note Only partial negation occurs when *not* is used with *all, both, every, whole, entirely, always, necessarily,* or *completely.*

a) I couldn't solve all the problems. Some of them were too difficult.

b) You don't necessarily have to attend the meeting.

Preposition

Into

Usage
into the goal
into new clothes
into the house
into the country

a) I saw the girl go into the store.

b) The water turned into ice.

c) She translated the novel into French.

Choose the correct word or phrase to complete each sentence.

Hint

1. We didn't go out because it was raining (heavy / heavily).

   was raining

2. I hate doing homework. I (rarely / frequently) try to avoid it.

   hate doing, avoid

3. Your writing is terrible. I can (hard / hardly) read it.

   can, read

4. I'm happy (to / that) see you.

   happy, see

5. The test was (surprising / surprisingly) easy.

   easy

6. The man became (violent / violently) when the waiter asked him to leave.

   became

7. She's always afraid (walks / to walk) alone at night.

   afraid

8. I know (both / all) of her parents.

   parents

9. I was shocked (that / to) he was promoted.

   he was promoted

10. I'm sure you are tired (of / for) doing this work.

    tired

Part 1 Picture Description

Listen and choose the statement that best describes the picture.

1.   (A)   (B)   (C)   (D)

2.   (A)   (B)   (C)   (D)

3.   (A)   (B)   (C)   (D)

4.  (A)   (B)   (C)   (D)

5. (A)   (B)   (C)   (D)

Part 2 Questions and Responses

Listen and choose the correct answer.

1. (A)   (B)   (C)
2. (A)   (B)   (C)
3. (A)   (B)   (C)
4. (A)   (B)   (C)
5. (A)   (B)   (C)

Listen and choose the correct answer.

1. Where is the man going?

   (A) Home
   (B) New York
   (C) To the bus terminal
   (D) To the ferry

2. What is the man doing?

   (A) Taking a bus from New Jersey
   (B) Taking a bus from New York
   (C) Taking a train to New York
   (D) Taking a bus to New Jersey

3. How much time does the man have?

   (A) One hour
   (B) Until tomorrow
   (C) Ten minutes
   (D) Twenty minutes

4. Who is Peter?

   (A) Sara's brother
   (B) Sara's friend
   (C) Sara's neighbor
   (D) Sara's uncle

5. Which of the following sentences is NOT true?

   (A) Peter is married.
   (B) Peter lives next to Sara.
   (C) Peter has no children.
   (D) Peter is a father.

6. How many people live in Peter's house?

   (A) One
   (B) Two
   (C) Three
   (D) Four

Listen and choose the best answer to each question.

1. What kinds of classes are being offered?

    (A) English classes   (B) Many different classes
    (C) Korean classes   (D) Cooking classes

2. What does the man say about Hondo classes?

    (A) They are exciting.   (B) They are easy.
    (C) They are fun.   (D) They are challenging.

3. On which day do the classes start earlier?

    (A) Monday
    (B) Sunday
    (C) Saturday
    (D) Tuesday

4. How long has the speaker been working at the zoo?

    (A) About ten years   (B) About fifteen years
    (C) Less than twenty years   (D) More than twenty years

5. What does the speaker like to do during her lunch break?

    (A) Walk around the zoo   (B) Run around the zoo
    (C) Walk around the park   (D) Feed the hippos

6. What is the speaker's favorite animal?

    (A) The hippo   (B) The penguin
    (C) The monkey   (D) The elephant

Choose the word or phrase that best completes the sentence.

1. During the party, ------- chairs got broken.

    (A) completely   (B) both
    (C) all of   (D) every

2. It was very ------- to meet you.

    (A) glad   (B) nice
    (C) happy   (D) interested

3. Is the store ------- on Sundays?

    (A) open   (B) opens
    (C) will open   (D) to opening

4. Our discussion turned ------- a big fight.

    (A) in   (B) to
    (C) at   (D) into

5. The wind is blowing ------- today.

    (A) difficult   (B) hard
    (C) difficulty   (D) hardly

6. He is always very -------.

    (A) patient   (B) patience
    (C) patiently   (D) impatiently

7. It's impossible ------- a penguin to fly.

    (A) to   (B) that
    (C) for   (D) if

8. That's the house ------- roof is leaking.

    (A) where   (B) into

    (C) that   (D) whose

9. The dishwasher is now -------.

    (A) hungry   (B) lonely

    (C) honest   (D) empty

10. I ------- to get off here. It's my stop.

    (A) shouldn't   (B) can

    (C) have   (D) usually

11. Neither of them know how to cook, so they ------- eat out.

    (A) often   (B) seldom

    (C) rarely   (D) never

12. My manager made a ------- announcement after the meeting.

    (A) surprised   (B) surprising

    (C) to surprise   (D) surprisingly

13. We gave a thank-you card ------- our teacher.

    (A) to   (B) with

    (C) for   (D) on

14. My mother bought a cell phone ------- my birthday present.

    (A) to   (B) at

    (C) in   (D) for

15. They went ------- Guam on vacation.

    (A) with   (B) to

    (C) for   (D) about

Part 6 Incomplete Texts

Choose the best word or phrase for each blank.

Questions 1 through 3 refer to the following note.

Allie,

Can you send Mrs. Sanders the new samples as soon as possible? She has called me
1. ------- every day this week, including Saturday, and I feel like I am being

    (A) most
    (B) almost
    (C) at most
    (D) almost all

2. ------- . She has already seen most of the samples in my catalog, but she wants

    (A) jumped
    (B) loaded
    (C) chased
    (D) marched

to see the newer materials. I have no time to fix something up myself, so I'd really
appreciate your **3.** ------- . There is a file on my desk with all the information.

        (A) help
        (B) helping
        (C) assist
        (D) assistant

Please take it if you need to check any details. Call me after you send the samples.

Thanks,
Ada

Questions 4 through 6 refer to the following advertisement.

Too busy to clean your home? Ashamed to invite people to visit? Then you need Homework Cleaners. The famous cleaning service is now available in your town. Our cleaners will march **4.** ------- your home and clean it up in no time at all. Our

    (A) by
    (B) in
    (C) into
    (D) along

cleaners can all be trusted to do a **5.** ------- job. Your house will be so clean, you won't

    (A) good
    (B) best
    (C) bad
    (D) poor

recognize it when you come home. We interview all staff very carefully, so you can feel assured that they will treat your home with respect. And, **6.** ------- prices are

    (A) we're
    (B) we
    (C) your
    (D) our

unbelievable. So give us a call today on 0334-778-3342 and find out more.

Choose the best answer.

<u>Questions 1 and 2</u> refer to the following newspaper article.

All the sports, all the time — World Wide Sports Center.

TODAY'S SPORTS SCORES

Baseball

Giants 7 - 3 Bluebirds
Lions   2 - 4 Yellow Socks
Bears   4 - 5 Tigers

In baseball today, Bluebirds and Lions fans were upset. The Giants crushed the Bluebirds, and the Yellow Socks beat the Lions. Tiger fans, though, were happy with their team's victory over the Bears.

Soccer

Tornadoes 0 - 2 Superstars

In soccer news, the Superstars won again — this time beating the Tornadoes. Way to go, Superstars!

1. Which teams won?

   (A) The Giants, the Lions, the Bears, and the Tornadoes
   (B) The Bluebirds, the Lions, the Bears, and the Tornadoes
   (C) The Giants, the Yellow Socks, the Tigers, and the Superstars
   (D) The Bluebirds, the Yellow Socks, the Tigers, and the Superstars

2. Which team is NOT a baseball team?

   (A) The Superstars   (B) The Yellow Socks
   (C) The Tigers   (D) The Bears

Questions 3 through 5 refer to the following letter.

Dear Susie,

How are you? I'm doing fine here at summer camp. We go swimming every day. At first, I was scared of the water. But now, after swimming lessons, I enjoy it. At night, we have a campfire. It's so pretty to look at. We usually sing songs and watch the stars until we fall asleep. I really enjoy that part of the day. I have met lots of really nice people, but I still miss home and all my friends.

See you in two weeks!

Your friend,
Jessica

3. Where is Jessica?

(A) At school
(C) At the movies
(B) At summer camp
(D) In the swimming pool

4. When will Susie see Jessica again?

(A) In a couple of weeks
(C) In a week
(B) In two days
(D) In one month

5. How does Jessica feel about the water?

(A) She feels scared.
(C) She thinks it is beautiful.
(B) She enjoys it.
(D) She thinks it is dangerous.

World Travel Co. — SPECIAL PRICES!

Ever wanted to see the Eiffel Tower? Walk along the Thames?
Shop in Seoul? Now you can with our summer deals!

From May 15th - June 30th only

Tokyo	- $699
Seoul	- $679
Rome	- $499
London	- $299
Paris	- $350

Book now for your summer vacation. Great deals on tours and flights.
Our well-trained agents can help you with all your travel needs!

Tax and other fees not included in price. To book online, go to www.wtc.com.

Memo
To: All agents
From: Head office
Re: New advertisement
Date: March 30th

Here are our special offers for the early summer period. Please put this poster in your store window. We will pay $10 commission for every customer who buys one of our summer deals. Let's try to break last year's sales record.

Good luck!

6. What is the most expensive trip?

   (A) Tokyo   (B) Seoul
   (C) Rome   (D) London

7. George has $300. Where can he go?

   (A) Seoul   (B) Rome
   (C) London   (D) Paris

8. On which date are special prices NOT available?

   (A) May 16th (B) May 30th
   (C) July 30th (D) June 1st

9. What will World Travel Co. give an agent who sells summer deals to twenty customers?

   (A) $10   (B) $20
   (C) $200   (D) Nothing

Comparisons

Vocabulary

A. LISTENING (Household)

Listen and write the letter of the statement that best describes the picture.

Exercise 1

1. _____ 2. _____ 3. _____ 4. _____

Exercise 1
1. (C) Clean   2. (D) Wash   3. (B) Cut   4. (A) Comb

Exercise 2

1. _____ 2. _____ 3. _____ 4. _____

Exercise 2
1. (C) Sweep   2. (D) Fold   3. (B) Polish   4. (A) Check

B. READING (Commonly Confused Words)

Choose the correct word to complete each sentence.

Exercise 1

1. I drank (fewer / less) tea today than yesterday.
2. These days, I work (fewer / less) hours.

Exercise 1
1. less   2. fewer

Exercise 2

1. The (object / subject) of today's class is Korean History.
2. What is that (object / subject) in your bag?

Exercise 2
1. subject   2. object

Exercise 3

1. Let's (raise / rise) that flag.
2. What time does the sun (raise / rise)?

Exercise 3
1. raise   2. rise

Comparisons

1. As ~ As comparison: as + adjective/adverb + as

   ▶ **Only the regular form of an adjective or adverb comes between *as* and *as*.**
   a) William is as more tall as his brother. (X) (more tall → tall)
   b) Gary is as smart as any boy in his class.
   c) Learning to play tennis is not as easy as it seems.

   ▶ **Multiplicative words (ex. twice, three times, etc.) are placed in front of the first *as*.**
   a) This is three times as large as that.
      (= This is three times larger than that.)
   b) Your car is twice as fast as my car.

2. Regular comparison

   ▶ **comparative form of adjective/adverb + than**
   a) This hotel is more expensive than that hotel.
   b) Gary is smarter than any other boy in his class.
   c) I have never been happier (than I am now).
   d) Of the two houses, this is the more beautiful.
      (When comparing between two, the comparative form is used with "the.")

   ▶ **Use *to* instead of *than* with the following adjectives: senior, junior, superior, inferior.**
   a) Your car is much superior to mine.
   b) In this company, she is senior to me.

   ▶ **Comparatives can be modified by the following words: much, even, far, still, a lot.**
   a) It is much colder today than it was yesterday.
   b) The sun rises even earlier in June.

3. Superlatives

   ▶ **"The" is used before a superlative. When there is no noun modified by the superlative, "the" can be omitted.**
   a) It was the cheapest car that I could find.
   b) Gary is the smartest boy in his class.
   c) He ran fastest of all.
   d) He is the most handsome teacher in the school.

P r e p o s i t i o n

Usage

on the beach
on Saturday
on time
on my street

On

a) Father will come back on Sunday.
b) Our vacation started on December 27th.
c) The post office is on Maple Street.

Grammar Exercises

Choose the correct word or phrase to complete each sentence.

Hint

1. Last night, I went to bed (early / earlier) than usual.

   than

2. It is (much / more) hotter on the sun than on the moon.

   hotter

3. This computer is inferior (to / than) that one.

   inferior

4. Taking the train is not (as / more) expensive as flying.

   not, expensive as

5. This section is (very / much) easier than the rest.

   easier

6. The cheetah is the (faster / fastest) animal in Africa.

   the, in Africa

7. That was (most / the most) delicious meal I've ever had.

   I've ever had

8. He is five years senior (to / than) me.

   ----

9. Of the two subjects, English is the (more / most) interesting.

   of the two

10. Gas is twice as expensive (as / than) it was a few years ago.

    as expensive

Part 1 Picture Description

Listen and choose the statement that best describes the picture.

1.   (A)   (B)   (C)   (D)

2.   (A)   (B)   (C)   (D)

3.   (A)   (B)   (C)   (D)

4.
(A)   (B)   (C)   (D)

5.   (A)   (B)   (C)   (D)

Part 2 Questions and Responses

Listen and choose the correct answer.

1.   (A)   (B)   (C)
2.   (A)   (B)   (C)
3.   (A)   (B)   (C)
4.   (A)   (B)   (C)
5.   (A)   (B)   (C)

Part 3 Short Conversations

Listen and choose the correct answer.

1. How much coffee does the woman drink every day?

   (A) Two cups (B) Three cups
   (C) Four cups (D) Five cups

2. What is the man's advice?

   (A) The woman should make coffee for her coworkers.
   (B) The woman should drink less coffee.
   (C) The woman shouldn't put sugar in her coffee.
   (D) The woman should find a new job.

3. Why does the woman drink so much coffee?

   (A) She really likes it. (B) It helps her focus on her work.
   (C) It keeps her awake. (D) She gets free coffee at work.

4. What are the man and woman discussing?

   (A) A party (B) Work
   (C) Time (D) Vacations

5. What time did the man arrive?

   (A) 10 p.m. (B) Not yet
   (C) After 10 p.m. (D) Before 10 p.m.

6. Why didn't the man see the woman?

   (A) She was in a different room. (B) She left before he arrived.
   (C) She wasn't invited. (D) She was hiding from him.

Listen and choose the best answer to each question.

1. How does the speaker get to work?

    (A) He drives to work.   (B) He walks.
    (C) He cycles.   (D) He takes a bus.

2. When does the speaker finish work?

    (A) 6:00   (B) 7:00
    (C) 8:00   (D) 9:00

3. Which activity does the speaker NOT do after work?

    (A) Go shopping   (B) Walk through the park
    (C) Play tennis   (D) Watch TV

---

4. What is on sale?

    (A) Pets   (B) Vehicles
    (C) Markets   (D) Bikes

5. What kind of cars does Bunny Motors sell?

    (A) Rich ones   (B) Cheap ones
    (C) Smart ones   (D) Expensive ones

6. How much can you save at Bunny Motors?

    (A) 50% or less   (B) 50% or more
    (C) Fifty times   (D) Fifty dollars

Choose the word or phrase that best completes the sentence.

1. I am taller ------- you.

   (A) as
   (B) than
   (C) more than
   (D) less than

2. A plane is ------- than a bus.

   (A) faster
   (B) more fast
   (C) more faster
   (D) fastest

3. This one is more ------- than that one.

   (A) cheap
   (B) cheaper
   (C) expensive
   (D) expensively

4. This lake is much ------- than the one near my house.

   (A) deep
   (B) deeper
   (C) deeply
   (D) deepness

5. This black wallet is much ------- attractive than the brown one.

   (A) too
   (B) more
   (C) so
   (D) as

6. The mummy is the ------- object in the museum.

   (A) interesting
   (B) boring
   (C) more interesting
   (D) most interesting

7. Her granddaughter is as tall ------- a high school student.

   (A) as
   (B) than
   (C) for
   (D) of

8. Misung swims ------- than Mia, but Mia can swim farther.

(A) fast
(B) faster
(C) fastest
(D) too fast

9. Brian is a lot ------- than George.

(A) taller
(B) the taller
(C) tall
(D) more taller

10. Sally is ------- more quickly than Steve.

(A) much
(B) runs
(C) the
(D) running

11. December 31ˢᵗ is the date ------- we meet every year.

(A) at which
(B) through
(C) on which
(D) where

12. I have ------- money now than I had last year.

(A) fewer
(B) much
(C) less
(D) a lot

13. Steve ------- been to Paris more often than Sally has.

(A) is
(B) has
(C) have
(D) at

14. Gary is late again. He's never ------- time!

(A) on
(B) at
(C) the
(D) rise

15. If you know the answer, please ------- your hand.

(A) yawn
(B) raise
(C) rise
(D) comb

Choose the best word or phrase for each blank.

<u>Questions 1 through 3</u> refer to the following advertisement.

The Best Shoes big sale is now on. We are offering our best ever prices for just one week. Come find the **1.** ------- shoes in town. You know we have the best quality,

      (A) biggest
      (B) more
      (C) cheapest
      (D) happiest

the friendliest staff, and the **2.** ------- location. So what are you waiting for? Come

      (A) best convenient
      (B) most convenient
      (C) more convenient
      (D) convenientest

to Best Shoes NOW! Get a free shoe brush with every pair of shoes you buy. We are located next to the central post office on Main Street. We **3.** ------- open from 10 a.m.

      (A) are
      (B) is
      (C) have
      (D) did

to 10 p.m. every day. See you soon.

To: Gwen Finch, Chris Goodwin
From: Michael Di Beni

Re: Deadline
Date: January 28th, 2007

Sorry, folks. This is just to let you know that the deadline for the new grammar book has been changed. The new deadline is much **4.** ------- than the old one, so you

(A) more soon
(B) soonest
(C) sooner
(D) sooner or later

will have to finish everything much **5.** ------- than you expected. The date has been

(A) quicker
(B) quickly
(C) quick
(D) as quick as

brought forward to March 13th, instead of May 2nd as originally planned. There is some good news, however. Because of the new deadline and the increased stress, you will be getting a raise. We will **6.** ------- you $200 more than normal. If the book

(A) raise
(B) earn
(C) support
(D) pay

is successful, you will have a permanent raise of $50 per month.

Choose the best answer.

Questions 1 and 2 refer to the following invitation.

Ms. Jennifer Smith and Mr. Michael Jones, together with their parents, are pleased to invite you to their wedding ceremony. The ceremony is at 3:00 p.m. on Saturday, November 22 at the Pleasantville Community Church on 23 Maple Street.

We have reserved a party room at O'Byrne's Pub at six o'clock for the reception. Please respond as soon as possible — if there are fewer than forty guests attending the reception, we can cancel the party room.

1. Where will the wedding reception be held?

(A) The Jones' house   (B) Pleasantville Community Church

(C) O'Byrne's Pub   (D) Maple Street

2. Which statement is NOT true?

(A) Jennifer and Michael are getting married.

(B) Their parents are getting married.

(C) They are getting married in a church.

(D) They are getting married on a Saturday.

Questions 3 through 5 refer to the following table.

	Boys	Girls
Asia	100	125
Australia	25	15
Europe	65	70
N. America	45	50
S. America	30	35

The students at the International Middle School come from many different places. There are boys and girls from around the world. In fact, there are more girls from Asia, Europe, North America, and South America than boys from these places. However, there are fewer girls from Australia than boys. In any case, the school is truly an international place!

3. Where do most of the students come from?

   (A) Asia
   (B) Australia
   (C) Europe
   (D) North America

4. Which is true?

   (A) There are more girls from South America than girls from Asia.
   (B) There are more girls from Asia than boys from Australia.
   (C) There are more boys from North America than girls from Europe.
   (D) There are more boys from South America than boys from North America.

5. How many students come from the United States and Canada?

   (A) None
   (B) 140
   (C) 95
   (D) 65

Department Store Directory

- 6th Floor Italian Restaurant and Coffee Shop
- 5th Floor Antique and Modern Furniture
- 4th Floor Books, Magazines, and Children's Clothing
- 3rd Floor Men's Clothing
- 2nd Floor Women's Clothing
- 1st Floor Computers and Home Electronics

Today's Value Club Cardholder's Specials: 40% off all his-and-hers cardigans (10:30-11:30), 2-for-1 spaghetti lunch set (11:30-13:30), 20% off all Pentium 5 desktop computers (all day).
Hours of operation: 9:30 a.m.-10:30 p.m.

To: Club Cardholders <club0223@laceys.co>
From: Laceys Department Store
Subject: Check out our changes
Date: January 30th

Dear Club Cardholder,

Here at Laceys, we've been trying to make our store even better. We have made a lot of changes and we would like to invite you to take a closer look. We have moved some of items, so take a look at the new directory. It will make your shopping easier the next time you visit.

Sincerely,

M. Morgan
Manager, Laceys Department Store

6. Where can you buy a table?

(A) On the 2nd floor   (B) On the 3rd floor
(C) On the 4th floor   (D) On the 5th floor

7. What can you buy on the 1st floor?

(A) A belt   (B) A sweater
(C) A DVD player   (D) A cup of coffee

8. When can a Value Club cardholder buy a sweater on sale?

(A) In the morning   (B) In the afternoon
(C) In the evening   (D) All day

9. Why did the manager of Laceys send this email?

(A) To tell customers about changes (B) To say hello
(C) To answer a complaint   (D) To tell customers that the store is closing

Vocabulary

A. LISTENING (Leisure II)

Listen and write the letter of the statement that best describes the picture.

Exercise 1

1. _____ 2. _____ 3. _____ 4. _____

Exercise 1
1. (C) Sing   2. (A) Paint
3. (D) Play   4. (B) Watch

Exercise 2

1. _____ 2. _____ 3. _____ 4. _____

Exercise 2
1. (A) Take a bath   2. (D) Lie
3. (B) Read   4. (C) Relax

B. READING (Commonly Confused Words)

Choose the correct word to complete each sentence.

Exercise 1

1. It is very (quiet / quite) tonight.
2. The moon was (quiet / quite) bright.

Exercise 1
1. quiet   2. quite

Exercise 2

1. The story is very (interested / interesting).
2. I am (interested / interesting) in the story.

Exercise 2
1. interesting   2. interested

Exercise 3

1. I want to (lay / lie) down. I'm tired.
2. Please (lay / lie) the book on the table.

Exercise 3
1. lie   2. lay

Grammar Focus

Conjunctions

1. Coordinating conjunctions (Tip-FANBOYS: for, and, nor, but, or, yet, so)

▶ **Addition/alternation**
a) She is playing the guitar and singing.
b) You can read a book or take a bath.
▶ **Contrast**
a) He is tall, but his son is short.
b) She is very rich, yet she doesn't wear expensive clothes.
▶ **Reason/result**
a) I bought a new tie, for I have a job interview tomorrow.
b) She saved money so she could go to Europe.

2. Subordinating conjunctions

when, after, before, since, as, until, as soon as

▶ **Simultaneous/sequential action**
a) Mary was listening to the radio while she was studying.
b) Sharapova has loved tennis since she was a child.
c) It was late by the time I got home.

if, unless, as long as

▶ **Condition**
a) As long as you promise to be back before nine, you can go out.
b) We will have fun at the beach, unless it rains.

though, although, even if, no matter what

▶ **Concession**
a) It is true, although it may sound strange.
b) Even if it snows, we must go to school.

because, since, as, in that

▶ **Reason**
a) Since you can't answer the question, we'd better ask someone else.
b) He ate a hamburger because he was hungry.

so that, in order that

▶ **Purpose**
a) David took a taxi so that he would be early.
b) In order that he not fail again, Garrett enrolled in a test prep course.

3. Correlative conjunctions

both...and, not only...but, whether...or, either...or, neither...nor

▶ **Inclusion**
a) She likes to play both football and hockey.
b) He studies not only English, but Spanish, too.
▶ **Exclusion**
a) Our milkshakes come in either chocolate or vanilla.
b) Neither my father nor I like watching the ballet.
c) It doesn't matter to me whether it rains or not.

Preposition

over the sea
over ten years ago
over the department
all over the world

Over

a) The plane was flying over the lake.
b) The war lasted over thirty years.
c) He has no control over himself.

Choose the correct word or phrase to complete each sentence.

1. Let's wait (by / until) it stops raining.

   wait, it stops

2. She was (quiet / quite) angry after the argument.

   angry

3. I thought that movie was very (interested / interesting).

   that movie

4. He went to (neither / either) the bank nor the post office.

   nor

5. We met a lot of nice people (during / while) our vacation.

   our vacation

6. I have known her (when / since) she was a child.

   have known

7. It was raining, (but / so) I brought my umbrella with me.

   raining, umbrella

8. I will lend you the money (as long as / although) you pay me back.

   ----

9. During our last vacation, we visited both London (and / or) Paris.

   both

10. (Yet / Although) it rained a lot, we enjoyed our vacation.

    rained, we enjoyed

Part 1 Picture Description

Listen and choose the statement that best describes the picture.

1.  (A)   (B)   (C)   (D)

2.   (A)   (B)   (C)   (D)

3.  (A)   (B)   (C)   (D)

4.    (A)   (B)   (C)   (D)

5.   (A)   (B)   (C)   (D)

Part 2 Questions and Responses

Listen and choose the correct answer.

1.   (A)   (B)   (C)
2.   (A)   (B)   (C)
3.   (A)   (B)   (C)
4.   (A)   (B)   (C)
5.   (A)   (B)   (C)

Listen and choose the correct answer.

1. Where does the man want to go?

(A) To the bookstore   (B) To the bank

(C) To the movies   (D) To the library

2. How can he get to the bank?

(A) Turn left, then go straight

(B) Go straight for two blocks, then turn left

(C) Go straight for one block, then turn left

(D) Go straight for one block then turn right

3. What does the woman say about the bookstore?

(A) That it has a wide variety of books

(B) That it is difficult to find

(C) That it is quite far away

(D) That the man might not find the book he needs

---

4. What is the man going to do after the conversation?

(A) Go home   (B) Take a bath

(C) Go to the supermarket   (D) Clean the bathroom

5. What does the woman want him to buy?

(A) Some towels   (B) A bath

(C) Some shampoo   (D) Some soap

6. What is the man worried about?

(A) The supermarket will be too crowded.

(B) He might buy the wrong soap.

(C) The woman will ask him to buy too many things.

(D) He thinks he might run out of money.

Listen and choose the best answer to each question.

1. How long has the speaker been studying judo?

   (A) Since he was ten
   (B) Before he was ten
   (C) Over ten years
   (D) After ten years

2. What happened to the speaker at his last competition?

   (A) He lost his match.
   (B) His opponent hurt his shoulder.
   (C) The referee studied judo.
   (D) He hurt his opponent's shoulder.

3. What did the speaker do to his opponent?

   (A) He punched him to the ground.
   (B) He kicked him to the ground.
   (C) He threw him to the ground.
   (D) He hurt his opponent's hand.

4. What does the speaker NOT have experience doing?

   (A) Cooking
   (B) Sweeping
   (C) Serving
   (D) Watering

5. When can the speaker start the new job?

   (A) Yesterday
   (B) A few years
   (C) This morning
   (D) Tomorrow

6. What does the speaker want?

   (A) Lunch in a restaurant
   (B) A new job
   (C) Some plants
   (D) Customers

Part 5 Incomplete Sentences

Choose the word or phrase that best completes the sentence.

1. I bought an umbrella ------- it was raining.

   (A) so   (B) because
   (C) also   (D) why

2. ------- you were a member, you could come too.

   (A) That   (B) If
   (C) Than   (D) So

3. ------- I was clean, I took a bath.

   (A) What   (B) As long as
   (C) Such   (D) Even though

4. I wanted to ------- down because I was quite tired.

   (A) lie   (B) bring
   (C) lay   (D) take

5. While ------- my new book, I learned something interesting.

   (A) to read   (B) read
   (C) to reading   (D) reading

6. ------- he was boarding the bus, he dropped his ticket in the gutter.

   (A) Whether   (B) How
   (C) While   (D) What

7. You can either rent ------- buy these skateboards.

   (A) or   (B) and
   (C) nor   (D) either

8. I neither registered for ------- attended the class.

    (A) or   (B) nor
    (C) either   (D) neither

9. I have been very tired -------.

    (A) late   (B) lately
    (C) sometime   (D) yet

10. ------- you hear the bell, you need to leave the classroom.

    (A) By the time   (B) As
    (C) Whether   (D) As soon as

11. She wore sunscreen ------- her skin would not burn.

    (A) because   (B) so
    (C) neither   (D) what

12. Yesterday, I went to school ------- bus.

    (A) over   (B) on
    (C) by   (D) with

13. My father has been working in the company ------- twenty years.

    (A) to   (B) over
    (C) at   (D) in

14. If I ------- help you, I would.

    (A) might   (B) do
    (C) shall   (D) could

15. When my friend opened the door, I walked ------- the house.

    (A) over   (B) into
    (C) for   (D) with

Choose the best word or phrase for each blank.

Questions 1 through 3 refer to the following memo.

Memo

To: Floor managers
From: Jake Spinner
Re: Factory changes

We are going to introduce a new system so that we can speed up production time. There will be a meeting **1.** ------- all the details are ready. When I have all the

    (A) as soon as
    (B) by
    (C) until
    (D) yet

information, I will announce a meeting time. We want to know your opinions, so no matter what, please don't hesitate to let us know **2.** ------- you think. We want

    (A) that
    (B) which
    (C) what
    (D) why

you to write down your ideas and give them to the systems control office. They will make a list of the **3.** ------- popular suggestions.

    (A) most
    (B) best
    (C) more
    (D) over

Questions 4 through 6 refer to the following letter.

Paper & Pens
Fancy Stationery
123 High Street
Wembley
Tel: 400-9945
May 3rd

Dear Mrs. Pemberton,

Thank you **4.** ------- your recent order. I am pleased to inform you that the items you

(A) over
(B) for
(C) with
(D) by

ordered are now available. Please call the store as soon as you get this letter. We will hold the items **5.** ------- June 3rd. However, if you we do not hear from you before

(A) until
(B) yet
(C) still
(D) since

then, we have to send them **6.** ------- to the supplier. Normally, we hold items for just

(A) in return
(B) as long as
(C) back
(D) in front

fourteen days, but since you are a regular customer, we are giving you a special extension.

Thank you, as always, for shopping at Paper & Pens.

Sincerely,
Cynthia Knowles,
Store manager

Choose the best answer.

<u>Questions 1 and 2</u> refer to the following letter.

Dear Grandma,

Thank you for the new bike that you gave me for my birthday. I am so happy it is blue, as that is my favorite color. Mom and Dad gave me money and some new clothes, and I got an interesting CD from Uncle Joe. I like your present the most, though. I ride it every day. I promise that I will take good care of it.

Love,
John

1.   What did John's grandmother give him?

(A) Money   (B) Clothes
(C) Roller skates   (D) A bicycle

2.   What does John promise to do?

(A) He promises to ride the bicycle every day.
(B) He promises to take care of the bicycle.
(C) He promises to spend his money wisely.
(D) He promises to write to his grandmother every day.

Questions 3 through 5 refer to the following notice.

> # Missing:
>
> ## Black-and-white Terrier named Sam
>
> He went missing on Tuesday, two days ago. We have been looking everywhere, but we can't find him. He is wearing a blue-and-red collar. We live near the park on King Street in Newtown. There is a reward for finding or helping us find Sam. He is our family pet. We have had him for six years.
>
> Please call Peter at 02-458-4879

3. On which day was the notice written?

(A) Tuesday (B) Wednesday
(C) Thursday (D) Friday

4. What color is the collar that Sam is wearing?

(A) Red-and-green (B) Green-and-blue
(C) Red-and-blue (D) Black-and-white

5. How long has the family owned Sam?

(A) Six years (B) Two days
(C) One year (D) Not long

Questions 6 through 9 refer to the following note and email.

Dear Frank,

My garden club meeting will finish late today, about an hour later than normal. After that, I have to go to the post office to buy some stamps. I will also get some milk because we have none left. Could you please start dinner? I will probably be too late to do it. If my brother calls, could you tell him that I will call him back tonight.

See you later,
Cindy

To: Cindy01@netnet.com
From: Frank22@netnet.com
Re: Dinner

Hey Cindy,

No problem. I will finish work a little earlier today so I can get dinner ready. How does spaghetti sound? Don't worry about milk. I will buy some on my way home.

Enjoy your club meeting. See you at home tonight.

Frank

6. What club does Cindy belong to?

   (A) The garden club   (B) The stamp-collecting club
   (C) The dinner club   (D) The movie club

7. Where does Cindy have to go after her meeting?

   (A) To the office   (B) To the bank
   (C) To the gas station   (D) To the post office

8. What should Frank do?

   (A) Take out the garbage   (B) Start dinner
   (C) Buy some stamps   (D) Go to the post office

9. After reading these emails, who is going to buy milk?

   (A) Cindy   (B) Frank
   (C) Both Frank and Cindy   (D) Neither Frank nor Cindy

Modifiers

Vocabulary

A. LISTENING (Passive Situations)

Listen and write the letter of the statement that best describes the picture.

Exercise 1

1. _____ 2. _____ 3. _____ 4. _____

Exercise 1
1. (B) Stand   2. (A) Hide   3. (D) Get up   4. (C) Wait

Exercise 2

1. _____ 2. _____ 3. _____ 4. _____

Exercise 2
1. (D) Look   2. (C) Listen   3. (B) Wear   4. (A) Rest

B. READING (Commonly Confused Words)

Choose the correct word to complete each sentence.

Exercise 1

1. I like the red shirt, and I like the blue one, (either / too).
2. I don't like the red shirt, and I don't like the blue one, (either / too).

Exercise 1
1. too   2. either

Exercise 2

1. She (looks / seems) very beautiful.
2. She (looks / seems) very kind.

Exercise 2
1. looks   2. seems

Exercise 3

1. The television is too loud. I can't (hear / listen) the radio.
2. He is clever. You should (hear / listen) to him.

Exercise 3
1. hear   2. listen

Grammar Focus

Modifiers

1. Words that modify the subject
   ▶ **verb + adjective**

   is (am, are), seem, appear, become, look, feel, sound, taste, smell

   a) He seems honestly. (X) (honestly → honest)
   b) The food tasted well. (X) (well → good)

2. Words that modify countable nouns: many, (a) few
   Words that modify uncountable nouns: much, (a) little

   a) Few students passed the exam.
   b) There was little time for study.

3. each, every + singular noun; each of + plural noun

   a) Each room has air conditioning.
   b) Each of the members did her best.

4. Use *some* in affirmative sentences and interrogative sentences that make a suggestion.
   Use *any* in interrogative sentences and negative sentences.

   a) I have any money. (X) (any → some)
   b) He didn't bring some books. (X) (some → any)
   c) Would you like some coffee?

5. such + a/an + adjective + noun; so + adjective + a/an + noun;
   so + adjective/adverb

   a) He's such a strong man (so strong a man) that he can carry the box.
   b) He's so strong that he can carry the box.
   c) She's so beautiful, and she can cook so well.

6. enough + noun; adjective + enough

   a) Linda saved enough money to buy a sports car.
   b) Linda is rich enough to buy a sports car.

7. almost + adjective; most + plural noun

   a) I go to the park almost every day.
   b) Most people who live there go to the park every week.
   c) Almost all the people who live there have been to the park.

8. -thing/-one/-body + adjective

   anything, everything, someone, everyone, nobody, anybody

   a) She would like to eat something warm.
   b) Can you suggest anyone suitable for this position?

Preposition

About

Usage

about 6:00
about history
about ten dollars
about the park

a) The book is about the Korean War.
b) He's arriving about two o'clock tomorrow.
c) I'm happy about his return.

Grammar Exercises

Choose the correct word or phrase to complete each sentence.

Hint

1. I feel (terribly / terrible) about the accident.

    feel

2. She bought a (real / really) beautiful dress.

    beautiful

3. (A number of / An amount of) students were wearing hats.

    students

4. Every (students / student) in the room has something to read.

    Every

5. He didn't have (some / any) money with him.

    didn't have

6. We have been waiting for a (such / very) long time.

    for a

7. Linda has (enough money / so money) to buy a big house.

    to buy

8. It's cold outside. I need (something warm / warm something) to wear.

    ----

9. (Almost / Most) people here can speak English well.

    people

10. She is (so / such) a smart student that she can enter the university.

    a smart student

Part 1 Picture Description

Listen and choose the statement that best describes the picture.

1.   (A)   (B)   (C)   (D)

2.   (A)   (B)   (C)   (D)

3.   (A)   (B)   (C)   (D)

4.    (A)   (B)   (C)   (D)

5.   (A)   (B)   (C)   (D)   

Part 2 Questions and Responses

Listen and choose the correct answer.

1.   (A)   (B)   (C)
2.   (A)   (B)   (C)
3.   (A)   (B)   (C)
4.   (A)   (B)   (C)
5.   (A)   (B)   (C)

Listen and choose the correct answer.

1. How much is a large envelope?

    (A) 75 cents   (B) 50 cents
    (C) 150 cents   (D) 10 cents

2. How many different types of envelopes are available?

    (A) Three   (B) Four
    (C) Five   (D) Six

3. How much would 100 small envelopes cost?

    (A) $45   (B) $50
    (C) $70   (D) $75

4. Where is this conversation taking place?

    (A) In an office   (B) At a sports center
    (C) At a railway station (D) In a department store

5. Where does the woman want to go?

    (A) To the shopping mall   (B) To the bank
    (C) To her mother's house (D) To Midland

6. Which train will the woman take?

    (A) The express because it is cheaper.
    (B) Neither, she will walk home.
    (C) Both of them
    (D) The local, because it is cheaper.

Listen and choose the best answer to each question.

1. Who do you think this ad is for?

    (A) People who have lots of energy
    (B) People who don't have much work
    (C) People who find it difficult to relax
    (D) People who are relaxed

2. How does yoga help people who work long days?

    (A) It gives them more energy.
    (B) It gives them a new job.
    (C) It doesn't help them.
    (D) It makes them stressed.

3. What days do the phones lines stay open?

    (A) Every day
    (B) Monday until Sunday
    (C) Every day except Tuesday
    (D) Every day except Monday

4. What did the speaker think of Canada?

    (A) She loved it.
    (B) She didn't like it.
    (C) She doesn't want to go back.
    (D) She hated it.

5. Who did the speaker walk in the mountains with?

    (A) Nobody
    (B) Her friends
    (C) Canada
    (D) Vacation

6. When did the speaker meet her friends for dinner?

    (A) In the mornings
    (B) Before her walks
    (C) After her walks
    (D) Two nights a week

Choose the word or phrase that best completes the sentence.

1. The food smells -------.

   (A) wonderfully   (B) well
   (C) very   (D) good

2. Alice goes to the movies about -------.

   (A) every two weeks   (B) every two week
   (C) every one week   (D) every once week

3. I hear ------- birds singing.

   (A) a little   (B) much
   (C) a lot of   (D) a great deal of

4. Would you like ------- tea?

   (A) many   (B) a few
   (C) a little   (D) every

5. I don't have enough time ------- for you.

   (A) wait   (B) waiting
   (C) to wait   (D) waited

6. She was ------- smart that she scored the highest on the test.

   (A) so   (B) very
   (C) enough   (D) too

7. She is ------- to music at the moment.

   (A) listens   (B) listening
   (C) hears   (D) hearing

8. There are ------- students waiting for their teacher.

(A) a little
(B) a few
(C) most
(D) almost

9. ------- students did their homework today.

(A) Most
(B) Almost
(C) Much
(D) Each

10. You seem ------- relaxing at the beach.

(A) enjoyed
(B) enjoying
(C) really enjoy
(D) to enjoy

11. He is much ------- in money than his brother is.

(A) for interested
(B) for interesting
(C) more interested
(D) more interesting

12. Can I borrow ------- money?

(A) most
(B) many
(C) a
(D) some

13. He ------- read twenty books about flying helicopters.

(A) has
(B) have
(C) so
(D) such

14. We have enough money to buy ------- ten hamburgers.

(A) into
(B) about
(C) with
(D) for

15. I really don't want anything to eat, -------.

(A) too
(B) so
(C) either
(D) such

Choose the best word or phrase for each blank.

<u>Questions 1 through 3</u> refer to the following message.

Lucy,

Can you ask the cleaner to empty all the trash cans before she goes home every night? **1.** ------- every morning this week, I have found the trash can in my office full

    (A) Most
    (B) At most
    (C) Almost all
    (D) Almost

of trash. Also, she should check that there is **2.** ------- toilet paper in the restrooms.

    (A) enough
    (B) such
    (C) each of
    (D) an

Last week, we ran out of toilet paper every day. It is very inconvenient and **3.** -------

    (A) everyone
    (B) no one
    (C) all
    (D) anyone

keeps complaining to me.

Thanks for your help,
Carrie

Computers Plus
34 West View Plaza
Tel: 887-9900
October 23rd

Dear Mr. Whitfield,

Thank you for your **4.** ------- letter. I am sorry that you have had problems with your

(A) lately
(B) new
(C) recent
(D) earlier

new Tondai Series-S laptop. We have had similar complaints from three other customers. We have **5.** ------- at your computer and tested it carefully. However, we

(A) checked
(B) looked
(C) listened
(D) waited

cannot find the cause of the trouble. We would like to exchange your computer for another. You may have either the same series again or a new computer from the T series.

Please contact me at the above telephone number, and let us know what you would like. I am very sorry for **6.** ------- inconvenience.

(A) that
(B) these
(C) those
(D) this

Sincerely,
Eric Winters

Choose the best answer.

<u>Questions 1 and 2</u> refer to the following sign.

NOTICE

Because of the Christmas and New Year holidays, the library will be closed December 24th-25th and December 31st-January 1st. In addition, our operating hours will be shortened to allow our staff more time with their families. Starting December 13th, we will be open from 9:00 a.m. to 4:30 p.m., from Monday to Friday. On Saturdays and Sundays, we will be open from 10:30 a.m. to 2:30 p.m. Our regular hours of operation will begin again on January 2nd.

1. On which day is the library open?

   (A) December 24th
   (B) December 26th
   (C) December 31st
   (D) January 1st

2. Why will the library be closed?

   (A) Because of the weather
   (B) Because of the new library
   (C) Because the librarian is sick
   (D) Because of the holidays

Questions 3 through 5 refer to the following menu.

Hilltop Restaurant
Menu

Hamburger (with lettuce, tomato, onion, and pickle)		$3.00
Cheeseburger (with cheddar cheese and bacon)		$3.50
Hotdog (with ketchup, mustard, and onion)		$2.00
Chili Hotdog (with ground beef and kidney beans)		$2.50
French Fries (regular or spicy fries)		$1.25
Onion Rings		$1.75
Soft Drinks (Cola, Lemon-Lime, Orange, Root Beer)	small	$1.25
	large	$1.50
Fresh Orange Juice or Lemon Iced Tea	small	$2.00
	large	$2.50

Please ask your server about today's specials.
Ask for our new dessert menu!

3. Which of the following is the most expensive?

   (A) A large cola   (B) French fries
   (C) A chili hotdog   (D) Onion rings

4. Mr. Smith bought two hamburgers and a hotdog. How much did he pay?

   (A) $6.00   (B) $5.50
   (C) $2.00   (D) $8.00

5. How many different kinds of drinks are on the menu?

   (A) Two   (B) Three
   (C) Five   (D) Six

Questions 6 through 9 refer to the following notice and text message.

We are sorry to report that Mr. Smith is sick today. Because of Mr. Smith's illness, his classes scheduled for today will be canceled: Beginning English, Advanced English, English Listening, and English Reading. Mr. Smith and the English department apologize for any inconvenience Mr. Smith's absence creates. Mr. Smith will be back tomorrow. Each student is responsible for reading the next chapter in his or her textbook. Please join us in wishing Mr. Smith a quick recovery.

Hey Jo! Did you see the notice? Mr. Smith is sick, so we've no class today. I'm so happy. I forgot to do my homework. Now I have an extra day. Let's talk about Jessie's party during class time. I don't want to read a boring book. Send me a reply! Sally

6. How many classes does Mr. Smith normally teach?

(A) Two   (B) Three
(C) Four   (D) Five

7. When will Mr. Smith be back?

(A) Today   (B) Tomorrow
(C) The day after tomorrow   (D) Next week

8. What should Mr. Smith's students do?

(A) They should come back next week.
(B) They should read the newspaper.
(C) They should buy their textbooks.
(D) They should read a chapter.

9. What will Sally probably do during class today?

(A) Write an essay   (B) Chat with her friend
(C) Read a book   (D) Take a nap

Negation

V o c a b u l a r y

A. LISTENING (Outdoors)

Listen and write the letter of the statement that best describes the picture.

Exercise 1

1. _____   2. _____   3. _____   4. _____

Exercise 2

   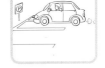

1. _____   2. _____   3. _____   4. _____

B. READING (Commonly Confused Words)

Choose the correct word to complete each sentence.

Exercise 1

1. The men (explored / exploded) the jungle.
2. The volcano (explored / exploded), and rocks flew into the air.

Exercise 2

1. I (wander / wonder) what he is doing now.
2. Let's (wander / wonder) through the park today.

Exercise 3

1. You must make a greater (afford / effort) to come to work on time.
2. I can't (afford / effort) the time away from work.

Exercise 1
1. (C) Walk   2. (D) Throw   3. (A) Water   4. (B) Climb

Exercise 2
1. (C) Pick   2. (A) Gather   3. (B) Dig   4. (D) Park

Exercise 1
1. explored   2. exploded

Exercise 2
1. wonder   2. wander

Exercise 3
1. effort   2. afford

Grammar Focus

Negation

1. Use *no* as an adjective.

   a) I have no equipment for mountain climbing.
   b) There are no bottles of juice in the fridge.

2. Use *not* as an adverb.

   ▶ *not* **can be used after auxiliaries and before main verbs.**

   a) She is not gathering enough berries.
   b) You should not walk on the grass.

   ▶ **If there is no auxiliary,** *do* **is used along with** *not*.

   a) I do not find this movie very interesting.
   b) She does not dig in the garden.

3. Put a negative word before non-finite verbs: to-infinitives, gerunds, and participles.

   a) We decided not to study French.
   b) I enjoy not waking up early in the morning.
   c) In order not to park downtown, he took a bus.

4. Never = not ever

   a) He never parks his car on the street.
   b) They can never pick enough apples.

   ▶ **The position of** *never* **changes the meaning of the sentence.**

   a) We decided never to climb Mt. Everest.
   b) We never decided to climb Mt. Everest.
   c) I enjoy never waking up early in the morning.
   d) I never enjoy waking up early in the morning.

5. Redundancy in Negation

   ▶ **Avoid double negatives.**

   a) I did not find no treasure. (X) (no → any)
   b) I found no treasure.

   ▶ **Do not use a negative word along with:** *hardly, seldom, rarely, scarcely, barely.*

   a) We could not hardly walk through the crowd. (X) Omit *not*
   → We could hardly walk through the crowd.

Preposition

Of

Usage

of wood
of the day
of America
of art

a) He is the owner of that big house.
b) They robbed him of his farm.
c) Her mother died of cancer.

Choose the correct word or phrase to complete each sentence.   Hint

1. There wasn't (no / any) gas in the car.   wasn't

2. She did (no / not) hear the truck explode.   did, hear

3. The police (never / not) found the missing hiker.   found

4. Bears (don't seldom / rarely) wander into town.   don't

5. She doesn't (want / not want) to explore the city   doesn't
    tomorrow.

6. We promised (to not / not to) speak in class anymore.   to speak

7. He (does not / not does) comb his hair very often.   comb

8. He can (afford not / not afford) to buy a bag of   can, not, diamonds
    diamonds.

9. I could (not barely / barely) hear the sound of music.   could, hear

10. You have (never / not never) been to London, have   -----------
    you?

Part 1 Picture Description

Listen and choose the statement that best describes the picture.

1.   (A)   (B)   (C)   (D)

2.   (A)   (B)   (C)   (D)

3.   (A)   (B)   (C)   (D)

4. (A) (B) (C) (D)

5. (A) (B) (C) (D)

Part 2 Questions and Responses

Listen and choose the correct answer.

1. (A) (B) (C)

2. (A) (B) (C)

3. (A) (B) (C)

4. (A) (B) (C)

5. (A) (B) (C)

Listen and choose the correct answer.

1. What are the man and woman doing?

    (A) Parking a car   (B) Buying a car
    (C) Looking for a friend   (D) Talking about space

2. Why is the man annoyed?

    (A) They wasted a lot of time.
    (B) He forgot to wear a watch.
    (C) The woman always wastes his time.
    (D) He hates parking.

3. What did it take them fifteen minutes to do?

    (A) Find the car   (B) Get ready
    (C) Get downtown   (D) Find a parking spot

4. Why is the woman angry?

    (A) She is always angry.
    (B) She was late for an appointment.
    (C) The man was late for their appointment.
    (D) She lost her handbag.

5. What time is it now probably?

    (A) 1:00 p.m.   (B) 2:00 p.m.
    (C) 2:30 p.m.   (D) 3:30 p.m.

6. Which sentence is probably true?

    (A) The man is often late.   (B) The man is never late.
    (C) The man has a car.   (D) The woman took the bus.

Listen and choose the best answer to each question.

1. If there is a fire, what should you do?

   (A) Run out of the building   (B) Stay seated
   (C) Walk out of the building   (D) Jog out of the building

2. When outside, where should you wait?

   (A) On the basketball court   (B) In the parking lot
   (C) Beside the school   (D) On the football field

3. How often will the fire drills be held?

   (A) Three times a year
   (B) Four times a year
   (C) Twice a year
   (D) Once each year

4. When should the students begin the test?

   (A) When they are given the test paper
   (B) When the teacher says paper
   (C) When they hear the bell
   (D) When they want

5. What should the students write on the first page?

   (A) Their teacher's name   (B) Their age
   (C) Their phone number   (D) Their name and class number

6. How much time do the students have to finish the test?

   (A) One hour   (B) Two hours
   (C) Three hours   (D) Five hours

Choose the word or phrase that best completes the sentence.

1. She never ------- mountains during the winter.

   (A) doesn't climb   (B) climbing
   (C) not climbs   (D) climbs

2. They prefer ------- through the streets at night.

   (A) walking not   (B) not to walking
   (C) not walking   (D) not walk

3. There are ------- workers picking cotton in the field.

   (A) not   (B) no
   (C) not never   (D) no never

4. He wandered ------- far that he forgot his way home.

   (A) very   (B) such
   (C) really   (D) so

5. Without effort, you ------- succeed in life.

   (A) will never   (B) never will
   (C) won't never   (D) never won't

6. Many people were killed when the ship ------- in the harbor.

   (A) explored   (B) been explored
   (C) exploded   (D) been exploded

7. ------- a tie, he couldn't enter the restaurant.

   (A) Not wearing   (B) Wearing not
   (C) Don't wear   (D) Wear not

8. Anna seemed happier ------- Wendy.

(A) as   (B) of
(C) over   (D) than

9. He seldom ------- ball with his children in the park.

(A) plays   (B) no plays
(C) doesn't play   (D) not plays

10. He ------- walk to work; he drives.

(A) no   (B) not
(C) does no   (D) does not

11. We can't afford ------- a new car.

(A) to buy   (B) buying
(C) buy   (D) do not buy

12. ------- of the squirrels are gathering nuts; those two are playing.

(A) Never all   (B) All never
(C) Not all   (D) All not

13. Her mother ------- to say that I had a heart of gold.

(A) have   (B) used
(C) was   (D) was used

14. He has never given me a box ------- chocolates.

(A) about   (B) of
(C) into   (D) in

15. I ------- believe how hard it was to pick apples.

(A) could hardly   (B) couldn't hardly
(C) hardly could   (D) hardly couldn't

Choose the best word or phrase for each blank.

Questions 1 through 3 refer to the following email.

To: sspt09@ccu.co
From: tatkins@netto.com
Subject: Contract
Date: June 3rd

Dear Mr. Conrad,

I am writing to you **1.** ------- the contract we made last week. In the contract, you

      (A) about
      (B) of
      (C) along
      (D) in

promised **2.** ------- use any workers without consulting me first. However, this morning

      (A) to not
      (B) to don't
      (C) to didn't
      (D) not to

I found two new workers on the building site. I **3.** ------- met them before, and I

      (A) am not
      (B) will not
      (C) had not
      (D) be not

was not told about them. I do not want a repeat of this. Please honor our contract.
I am very disappointed by this.

Tom Atkins

Questions 4 through 6 refer to the following advertisement.

Tired **4.** ------- your image? Fed up with your hair style? Don't want to wear the same

    (A) by
    (B) of
    (C) from
    (D) to

old clothes again and again? Then you need 'Image Over.' We advise clients on how to make the most of their appearance. Don't want to spend a lot of money on clothes and make-up? No problem. You don't have to be rich to look good. We can show you cheap and easy ways to improve your appearance and create a new look. Call 435-945 to make an appointment. One of **5.** ------- specialists will visit your home

    (A) us
    (B) ours
    (C) our
    (D) mine

and check your clothes and make-up. Then, the specialist will take you on a fun shopping trip to **6.** ------- you find things to improve your look. Call now and start

    (A) help
    (B) show
    (C) make
    (D) do

looking great!

Choose the best answer.

Questions 1 and 2 refer to the following menu.

Blue Coffee Shop

Hours of operation:
Monday to Friday: 6:00 a.m. to 11:00 p.m.
Saturdays: 8:00 a.m. to 10:00 p.m.
Sundays: 9:00 a.m. to 9:00 p.m.

MENU

Coffee (Colombian, Java, Kenyan)... $2.50
Tea (Earl Grey, Orange Pekoe, Darjeeling, Chai Spice)......... $2.00
Iced Tea (Lemon, Peach, Raspberry) $1.50
Fresh Juice (Orange, Apple, Grape, Grapefruit)................... $1.50
Hot Chocolate, Hot Caramel $2.50
Iced Chocolate, Iced Caramel... $2.25

2%, 1%, or nonfat milk available

1. Which is the most expensive?

   (A) Colombian coffee   (B) Darjeeling tea
   (C) Grape juice   (D) Lemon iced tea

2. Mr. and Mrs. Smith bought a cup of coffee and a glass of iced tea. How much did they spend?

   (A) $6.00   (B) $3.00
   (C) $4.00   (D) $5.50

Questions 3 through 5 refer to the following sign.

WELCOME TO CLUB DAY!

Flower Club Meeting

- Green thumbs, flower lovers, and romantics alike will enjoy this club. Meeting today at 4:00 p.m. in Room 330 of Charlton Hall.

Stamp Club Meeting

- Travel the world and swap valued stamps with fellow collectors. Meeting today at 4:30 p.m. in Room 304 of Janzen Hall.

Comics Club Meeting

- Relive tales of all your favorite Superfriends with fellow comic book lovers. Meeting this evening at 7:30 p.m. in Room 717 of O'Byrne Hall.

Coin Club Meeting

- Our newest club! Come swap coins from around the world. See examples of old coins and new coins, and notes from every corner of the globe. Meeting tonight at 8:00 p.m. in Room 210 of the newly built Ayres Hall.

3. What time is the flower club meeting?

(A) 3:30 p.m.   (B) 3:04 a.m.

(C) 4:00 p.m.   (D) 4:30 p.m.

4. Where is the stamp club meeting?

(A) Room 330   (B) Room 304

(C) Room 400   (D) Room 430

5. Which building was built most recently?

(A) Charlton Hall   (B) Janzen Hall

(C) O'Byrne Hall   (D) Ayres Hall

Questions 6 through 9 refer to the following emails.

From: Sue <sues@hanmail.com>
Sent: May 23rd
To: funnyboy <george@yahoo.ca>
Subject: pics

Hi there, George! Thanks for sending those pictures. Your new daughter is so cute! She was born last month, wasn't she? What does her older brother think of her? Is he happy to have a sister? Even if he isn't now, I'm sure he will be later. Anyway, I should get back to work. Keep those pictures coming.

Love,
Sue

From: funnyboy <george@yahoo.ca>
Sent: May 23rd
To: Sue <sues@hanmail.com>
Subject: Re:pics

Hi Sue,
Glad you liked the pictures. David loves his new sister. He wants to play with her all the time. He can't understand why she can't talk yet! I'll be sending a lot more pictures, so you can look forward to those. This office is so busy today. We have some important clients visiting. We'd like to invite you and Morris to come over some time.

Take care,
George

6. When was George's daughter born?

(A) This month   (B) Yesterday
(C) May   (D) April

7. How many children does George have?

(A) One   (B) None
(C) Two   (D) Three

8. What did George send Sue?

(A) A card   (B) Photos
(C) A gift   (D) A phone message

9. Where is George probably writing this email?

(A) At work   (B) In a public library
(C) In an Internet café (D) At home

Practice Test

LISTENING TEST

In the Listening test, you will be asked to demonstrate how well you understand spoken English. The entire Listening section of the test will last approximately 45 minutes. Directions are given for each of the four parts. There is a separate answer sheet for marking answers. Do not write your answers in the test book.

Part 1

Directions: In this part of the test, you will hear four statements about each picture in your textbook. After listening to all four statements, you must select the one statement that best describes what you see in the picture. Then, find the number of that question on your answer sheet and mark your answer. The statements will be spoken only one time, and are not printed in your test book.

Sample Answer

Ⓐ ● Ⓒ Ⓓ

Example

Now listen to the four statements.

Statement (B), "The woman is typing on a computer," best describes what you see in the picture. Therefore, you should choose answer (B).

1.

2.

GO ON TO THE NEXT PAGE ▶

3.

4.

5.

6.

GO ON TO THE NEXT PAGE ▶

7.

8.

9.

10.

GO ON TO THE NEXT PAGE ➤

Part 2

Directions: In this section you will hear a question or statement followed by three responses. Select the best response to the question or statement and mark the letter (A), (B), or (C) on your answer sheet. Again, each response will be spoken only one time and will not be printed in your test book.

Example

Sample Answer
● Ⓑ Ⓒ

You will hear: How are you today?

You will also hear: (A) I'm fine, thank you.
                       (B) It's cold, isn't it?
                       (C) Well, it's a difficult issue.

The best response to the question "How are you today?" is choice (A), "I'm fine, thank you." Therefore, you should choose answer (A).

11. Mark your answer on your answer sheet.

12. Mark your answer on your answer sheet.

13. Mark your answer on your answer sheet.

14. Mark your answer on your answer sheet.

15. Mark your answer on your answer sheet.

16. Mark your answer on your answer sheet.

17. Mark your answer on your answer sheet.

18. Mark your answer on your answer sheet.

19. Mark your answer on your answer sheet.

20. Mark your answer on your answer sheet.

21. Mark your answer on your answer sheet.

22. Mark your answer on your answer sheet.

23. Mark your answer on your answer sheet.

24. Mark your answer on your answer sheet.

25. Mark your answer on your answer sheet.

26. Mark your answer on your answer sheet.

27. Mark your answer on your answer sheet.

28. Mark your answer on your answer sheet.

29. Mark your answer on your answer sheet.

30. Mark your answer on your answer sheet.

31. Mark your answer on your answer sheet.

32. Mark your answer on your answer sheet.

33. Mark your answer on your answer sheet.

34. Mark your answer on your answer sheet.

35. Mark your answer on your answer sheet.

36. Mark your answer on your answer sheet.

37. Mark your answer on your answer sheet.

38. Mark your answer on your answer sheet.

39. Mark your answer on your answer sheet.

40. Mark your answer on your answer sheet.

Part 3

Directions: In this section of the test, you will hear a number of conversations between two people. You will be asked to answer three questions about what is said in each conversation. You must select the best response to each question and mark the letter (A), (B), (C), or (D) on your answer sheet. Each conversation will be spoken only one time and will not be printed in your test book.

41. Why is the woman going to travel?

(A) To go shopping
(B) To attend a conference
(C) To take a rest
(D) To eat some ice cream

42. Where will the woman travel to?

(A) Nowhere
(B) Her office
(C) New York
(D) We don't know

43. On what day does the conversation take place?

(A) Tuesday
(B) Wednesday
(C) Thursday
(D) Friday

44. How many sisters does John have?

(A) None
(B) Two
(C) Three
(D) Four

45. How many children do John's parents have?

(A) Three
(B) Four
(C) Seven
(D) Eight

46. How many younger sisters does John have?

(A) None
(B) One
(C) Two
(D) Three

47. What does Tom's brother do?

(A) He's a doctor.
(B) He's a pilot.
(C) He's a fireman.
(D) He's a dentist.

48. Why is the woman surprised?

(A) Her father is a fireman.
(B) She wants to be a doctor.
(C) Her brother used to be a doctor.
(D) Her brother is a fireman, too.

49. What does Tom think is possible?

(A) Tom knows the woman's brother.
(B) Tom's brother knows the woman's brother.
(C) Tom has a sister.
(D) The woman will become a doctor.

50. Why does the man think it will rain?

(A) He read the weather forecast.
(B) There a lot of black clouds.
(C) He can see many people with umbrellas.
(D) It has been raining all day.

51. What is the woman's problem?

(A) She doesn't want her new shoes to get wet.
(B) She missed the bus.
(C) She doesn't have an umbrella.
(D) She hates the rain.

52. What will the man do?

(A) Lend the woman an umbrella.
(B) Give the woman a ride home.
(C) Give the woman a ride to the station.
(D) Check the weather forecast.

GO ON TO THE NEXT PAGE

53. Why doesn't the woman have any money?

(A) She has a lot of debts.
(B) Her wallet was stolen.
(C) She forgot her wallet.
(D) She lost her wallet on the bus.

54. How much money will the man lend her?

(A) None. She should be more careful.
(B) As much as she wants.
(C) $50
(D) $500

55. When will the woman pay him back?

(A) Never
(B) On pay day
(C) Tomorrow
(D) In a week

56. What are the man and woman discussing?

(A) Their parents
(B) Their jobs
(C) House prices
(D) A sofa

57. Which of the following does the woman admire?

(A) The man's mother
(B) The color of his sofa
(C) The man's house
(D) The man's boss

58. What does the man say he will do?

(A) Ask his mother for some information
(B) Invite the woman to his mother's house
(C) Hold a dinner party
(D) Buy a new sofa

59. What does the woman want?

(A) Her cell phone
(B) A telephone number
(C) The man's cell phone
(D) A ride to the station

60. Who is the woman meeting?

(A) Her mother
(B) Her sister
(C) Her friend
(D) Her husband

61. What is the woman's problem?
(A) She can't remember where she has to go.
(B) She is going to be late.
(C) She has lost a report.
(D) She has a toothache.

62. When is the woman going on vacation?

(A) Later today
(B) Tomorrow
(C) Next week
(D) She is not going on vacation.

63. What does the woman need to buy?

(A) A suitcase
(B) New clothes
(C) A pair of shoes
(D) A birthday gift

64. Where does the man suggest the woman go shopping?

(A) In New York
(B) At the shopping mall
(C) At a department store
(D) At the supermarket

65. What had the man lost?

(A) A file
(B) His battery
(C) His car keys
(D) His cell phone

66. Where did the woman find it?

(A) Next to her cell phone
(B) Under a file
(C) Under the battery
(D) In a box

67. Why didn't the woman hear the phone ring?

(A) She has a hearing problem.
(B) She had been on vacation.
(C) The battery was dead.
(D) She didn't recognize the sound.

68. What did the man do yesterday?

(A) He found a new job.
(B) He quit his job.
(C) He gave the woman a job.
(D) He was fired by his boss.

69. How does the woman react?

(A) She is nervous.
(B) She is surprised.
(C) She is angry.
(D) She is happy.

70. Which of the following is probably true?

(A) The man is a good cook.
(B) The man will take a vacation.
(C) The man will quit his job.
(D) The man will look for a new job.

GO ON TO THE NEXT PAGE

Part 4

Directions: In this section of the test, you will hear a number of short talks given by a single speaker. Again, you must answer three questions about what is said in each talk. Choose the most appropriate response to each question and mark the letter (A), (B), (C), or (D) on your answer sheet. Each talk will be spoken only one time and will not be printed in your test book.

71. Where is this announcement being made?

(A) At an airport
(B) In a department store
(C) In a children's hospital
(D) At a playground

72. How much will a $50 sweater cost now?

(A) $50
(B) $5
(C) $15
(D) $25

73. Who would be most interested in this announcement?

(A) Children
(B) Tourists
(C) Parents
(D) Doctors

74. What is the next stop?

(A) Main Road
(B) Main Station
(C) Main Street
(D) Main Row

75. What line leads to Seoul soccer stadium?

(A) The brown line
(B) The green line
(C) The white line
(D) The purple line

76. What number is the white line?

(A) Number six
(B) Number four
(C) Number seven
(D) Number three

77. Where was the dog lost?

(A) Near the park
(B) Outside the city
(C) In the city center
(D) At the beach

78. What color is the dog?

(A) White with brown paws
(B) Brown with white paws
(C) Brown with black paws
(D) Black with brown paws

79. How much money will be given for help in finding the dog?

(A) Fifteen dollars
(B) Twenty dollars
(C) Thirty dollars
(D) Fifty dollars

80. How many people were in the raft?

(A) Ten
(B) Eleven
(C) Eight
(D) Nine

81. Where did they go for food afterwards?

(A) A Mexican restaurant
(B) An Italian restaurant
(C) A Spanish restaurant
(D) A French restaurant

82. What did the speaker think of the day?

(A) He thought it was strange.
(B) He thought it was boring.
(C) He thought it was great fun.
(D) He thought it was unexciting.

83. According to the weather report, where will the rain be?

(A) In the south
(B) In the east
(C) In the north
(D) In the west

84. How high will the temperatures reach in the north?

(A) 20 degrees
(B) 23 degrees
(C) 30 degrees
(D) 25 degrees

85. What difference will be seen between Monday and Tuesday?

(A) Monday will be far hotter.
(B) Tuesday will have more rain.
(C) There will be some higher temperatures on Tuesday.
(D) There will be some extra rain showers on Monday.

86. What does Dave's English camp try to do?

(A) To make English easy
(B) To make English fun
(C) To make English boring
(D) To help you write English

87. What time are the classes?

(A) From 8-11
(B) From 9-12
(C) From 7-12
(D) From 8-12

88. What can you do after class?

(A) Practice writing English
(B) Practice speaking English
(C) Watch English movies
(D) Do an English test

89. What does the speaker's cousin do?

(A) He takes pictures.
(B) He sells cameras.
(C) He is a movie star.
(D) He doesn't have a job.

90. How much has the speaker's cousin spent on his camera?

(A) Over two thousand dollars
(B) Over four thousand dollars
(C) Over three thousand dollars
(D) Over four hundred dollars

91. Who does he sell the photographs to?

(A) Book publishers
(B) Magazines
(C) Newspapers
(D) The local news station

92. How many people ran in the marathon?

(A) 20,000
(B) 30,000
(C) 200,000
(D) 300,000

93. Where will the money go?

(A) To the city parks
(B) To the city schools
(C) To the government
(D) To the city hospital

94. What time did the winner finish in?

(A) Two hours
(B) Two hours, thirty minutes
(C) Three hours
(D) Two hours, fifty minutes

GO ON TO THE NEXT PAGE ▶

95. Why are the students being sent home?

(A) It is a school holiday.
(B) There is a problem with the heating system.
(C) Some of the teachers are absent.
(D) The water pipes burst.

96. When will the buses arrive?

(A) In twenty minutes
(B) In thirty minutes
(C) In forty minutes
(D) In one hour

97. How will the students know if the school is closed the following day?

(A) Their parents will be called.
(B) It will be announced on the local TV station.
(C) They can find out on the Internet.
(D) The local radio station will make an announcement.

98. Where is this announcement most likely being made?

(A) On a train
(B) On the subway
(C) On an airplane
(D) On a boat cruise

99. Why do the passengers have to fasten their seatbelts?

(A) They are landing.
(B) Lunch is being served.
(C) They are taking off.
(D) They are passing through some rough weather.

100. What will happen in thirty minutes?

(A) They will land.
(B) Dinner will be served.
(C) They will enter into some bad weather.
(D) Lunch will be served.

This is the end of the listening part of the test. Turn to Part 5 in your test book.

NO TEST MATERIAL ON THIS PAGE

GO ON TO THE NEXT PAGE

READING TEST

In the Reading test, you will be required to answer several types of reading comprehension questions based on a variety of texts. The Reading section of the test will last 75 minutes. There are three parts, and directions are given for each part. You are encouraged to answer as many questions as possible within the time allowed.

You must mark your answers on the separate answer sheet. Do not write your answers in the test book.

Part 5

Directions: In each question, you will find a word or phrase missing. Four answer choices are given below each sentence. You must choose the best answer to complete the sentence. Then mark the letter (A), (B), (C), or (D) on your answer sheet.

101. Those are ------- books.

(A) her
(B) hers
(C) she's
(D) she

102. I'm ------- sick.

(A) feel
(B) feels
(C) feeling
(D) felt

103. ------- going to the soccer game.

(A) Their
(B) There
(C) They're
(D) There're

104. I have ------- friends.

(A) much
(B) many
(C) any
(D) most

105. Would you like something -------?

(A) drink
(B) drinks
(C) to drink
(D) to drinks

106. Can I borrow ------- money?

(A) a
(B) some
(C) most
(D) many

107. I don't have ------- money.

(A) any
(B) an
(C) a
(D) many

108. She has ------- eyes.

(A) beauty
(B) beautiful
(C) a beauty
(D) a beautiful

109. My mother ------- in a bank.

(A) work
(B) works
(C) working
(D) worker

110. I've been learning English ------- three years.

(A) for
(B) since
(C) while
(D) in

111. Where ------- he work?

(A) is
(B) are
(C) do
(D) does

112. Honey is made ------- bees.

(A) from
(B) to
(C) by
(D) out of

113. ------- is fun.

(A) Swimming
(B) A swimming
(C) Swim
(D) Be swimming

114. What are you ------- next weekend?

(A) do
(B) doing
(C) did
(D) done

115. Do you have ------- computer at home?

(A) a
(B) an
(C) some
(D) those

116. I usually ------- the bus to school.

(A) take
(B) takes
(C) take on
(D) takes on

117. We ------- to go shopping.

(A) enjoy
(B) must
(C) need
(D) couldn't

118. He works ------- a doctor in that hospital.

(A) at
(B) as
(C) and
(D) any

119. We enjoy ------- in the mountains.

(A) hike
(B) to hike
(C) hiking
(D) to hiking

120. She's waiting ------- her friend.

(A) to
(B) for
(C) about
(D) because

GO ON TO THE NEXT PAGE

121. I have no money. I'm -------.

(A) broke
(B) broken
(C) breaking
(D) break

122. That movie was very -------.

(A) interest
(B) interested
(C) interesting
(D) to interest

123. We've lived here ------- ten years.

(A) since
(B) during
(C) from
(D) for

124. She is the teacher ------- helped me.

(A) who
(B) when
(C) whose
(D) what

125. They hope ------- to Singapore next year.

(A) travel
(B) travels
(C) traveling
(D) to travel

126. ------- my friends take music lessons.

(A) Any
(B) Many
(C) Any of
(D) Many of

127. We don't have ------- problems.

(A) a
(B) any
(C) no
(D) none

128. They have not finished the project -------.

(A) already
(B) soon
(C) yet
(D) before

129. Sue always ------- a walk in the morning.

(A) takes
(B) makes
(C) goes
(D) does

130. The wind is blowing ------- today.

(A) difficult
(B) hard
(C) difficulty
(D) hardly

131. She ------- two brothers.

(A) have
(B) has
(C) does
(D) do

132. Put the milk ------- the top shelf of the fridge.

(A) on
(B) in
(C) over
(D) behind

133. What ------- you do yesterday?

(A) are
(B) were
(C) do
(D) did

134. Oops! I ------- a mistake!

(A) did
(B) made
(C) said
(D) get

135. Please wait ------- me.

(A) in
(B) over
(C) to
(D) for

136. ------- you like strawberry ice cream?

(A) Do
(B) Can
(C) Are
(D) Won't

137. My favorite color is -------.

(A) grapes
(B) apple
(C) orange
(D) pear

138. Are ------- your shoes?

(A) this
(B) these
(C) that
(D) them

139. He ------- milk every day.

(A) eats
(B) plays
(C) sits
(D) drinks

140. We like to ------- tennis.

(A) play
(B) plays
(C) playing
(D) played

GO ON TO THE NEXT PAGE

Part 6

Directions: Read the texts on the following pages. You will find a word or phrase missing in some of the sentences. Below each of the sentences, four answer choices are given. Select the most appropriate answer to complete the text. Then mark the letter (A), (B), (C), or (D) on your answer sheet.

Dear Sally,

I am going to **141.** ------- grandmother's house this afternoon. I will be out

        (A) the
        (B) our
        (C) your
        (D) yours

when you get home from school, so you will need to get your own dinner.
Help yourself **142.** ------- anything in the refrigerator. There is some cheese

        (A) with
        (B) to
        (C) by
        (D) over

and plenty of vegetables. There is bread, too. You can pick **143.** ------- apples

        (A) any
        (B) some
        (C) all
        (D) almost

from the tree in the garden if you want. As a special treat, I have bought
some chocolate fudge ice cream. Don't eat too much – I want to try some, too!
Do your homework, OK? I'll be home about eight o'clock. See you later.

Mom

GO ON TO THE NEXT PAGE

Memo

To: Sales Staff
From: Marketing
Re: Christmas sales target
Date: October 15th

It is time to start thinking **144.** ------- our Christmas sales. Last year, we saw

(A) on
(B) about
(C) for
(D) off

very low profits, so we really need to improve things this year. The store wants to double its profits, so we have a lot of work to do. We will have a meeting next Tuesday at three o'clock to discuss this. Please think of some good ideas to increase sales. If we reach the new target, **145.** ------- will get a bonus.

(A) everyone
(B) no one
(C) anyone
(D) each

If we are not successful, there will be no bonuses. The store manager will come to the meeting. He is going to **146.** ------- us his ideas and listen to our opinions.

(A) say
(B) talk
(C) tell
(D) speak

This is a very important meeting. Don't miss it.

Getaway Tours

We now have the details of our Summer Specials. As always we have some real treats. Just take a look at a sample of **147.** ------- we have on offer this year: six

    (A) that
    (B) what
    (C) which
    (D) why

nights in Guam, staying in a luxury hotel with breakfast included — starts at just $50 per person per night. Five nights in Hong Kong, staying in a 5 star hotel, including a guided harbor boat cruise -- starts at just $75 per person per night. **148.** ------- of our prices include travel insurance and free transportation

    (A) Almost
    (B) All
    (C) Nearly
    (D) At all

from the airport **149.** ------- to your hotel. Give us a call at 234-0009 for

    (A) straightly
    (B) directly
    (C) firstly
    (D) immediate

reservations or further information.

GO ON TO THE NEXT PAGE

To: Nina Tendo <ninten@cosmo.net>
From: Jane Sims <jsims@united_foods.co>
Subject: Customer Complaint #00234
Date: May 25th

Dear Ms. Tendo,
Thank you for your email last week. I am very sorry to hear that you had a problem with a United Foods product. You **150.** ------- us that you found ants in

(A) identified
(B) informed
(C) information
(D) identify

a packet of Jolly Cowboy cookies. We went to the store where you bought the cookies. We found ants in several packets of Jolly Cowboy cookies. We found that ants had entered the store room. We treated the problem, and there are **151.** ------- ants in the store room. We are very sorry that this happened, and

(A) not more
(B) more
(C) no more
(D) any more

hope you will continue to buy our food products. I am sending you a $20 coupon, **152.** ------- you can print out and use in any store to buy United Foods

(A) which
(B) what
(C) where
(D) who

products.

Sincerely,
Jane Sims
Customer Service Manager

Part 7

Directions: In this part of the test, you will read a selection of texts, such as magazine and newspaper articles, letters, and advertisements. Each text is followed by several questions. Choose the correct answer to each question and mark the letter (A), (B), (C), or (D) on your answer sheet.

GO ON TO THE NEXT PAGE

CAUTION: DETOUR

Drive Slowly

Due to the recent cold and snow resulting in dangerous
driving conditions on the Bukowski Bridge,
Route 66 is now closed to traffic.

All traffic going south on Route 66 must now travel
east on Route 75 to Williamsburg and
then turn south on Route 19.

Remember: Speed kills, so drive safely!

Happy holidays and thank you for your cooperation,

State Highway Department

153. Where would you probably see this sign?

(A) On a beach
(B) On a building
(C) In a forest
(D) Next to a highway

154. When would this sign probably be posted?

(A) In a rain storm
(B) In summer
(C) In winter
(D) On Saturday

Questions 155 and 156 refer to the following letter.

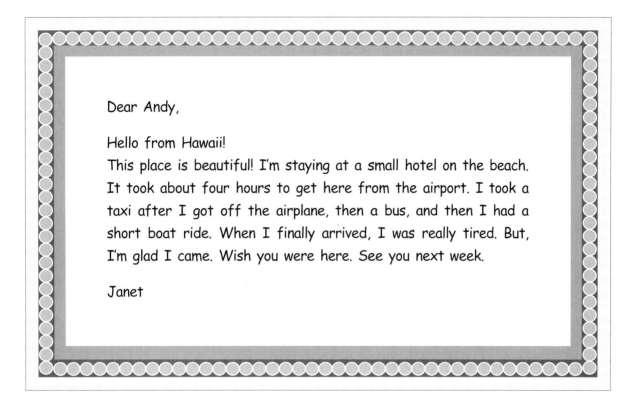

Dear Andy,

Hello from Hawaii!
This place is beautiful! I'm staying at a small hotel on the beach.
It took about four hours to get here from the airport. I took a
taxi after I got off the airplane, then a bus, and then I had a
short boat ride. When I finally arrived, I was really tired. But,
I'm glad I came. Wish you were here. See you next week.

Janet

155. Where is Janet staying?

(A) In a taxi
(B) In an airplane
(C) In a hotel
(D) In a tent

156. How did she travel there?

(A) First by taxi, then by bus, then by airplane
(B) First by airplane, then by taxi, then by bus, then by boat
(C) First by airplane, then by boat
(D) First by boat, then by bus, then by taxi

GO ON TO THE NEXT PAGE

Questions 157 through 159 refer to the following advertisement.

Always tired? No energy?

Do you need a little extra strength to get through that tough workday?

If you answered "yes," then try Vitagetic, the new energy drink.

Vitagetic has all the vitamins that your body needs to maintain a high level of energy all day long. It is an easy way to get all your vitamins. You don't have to take lots of vitamin pills. It comes in three fantastic flavors: Lemon, Orange, and Apple, and tastes great.

Have one bottle at breakfast and you will feel healthy and energetic until quitting time. You can find it at all good supermarkets.

157. Who should drink Vitagetic?

(A) People who are often tired
(B) People who have a lot of energy
(C) People who are bored
(D) People who can't sleep

158. Why is Vitagetic good for you?

(A) Because it has oranges and apples
(B) Because it has vitamins
(C) Because it comes in a bottle
(D) Because you drink it at breakfast

159. Which of the following is NOT true?

(A) You have to take vitamin pills with Vitagetic.
(B) You can buy Vitagetic at supermarkets.
(C) Vitagetic is a good breakfast drink.
(D) Vitagetic is delicious.

Questions 160 through 162 refer to the following sign.

Recycling Instructions

Please separate your trash into the following bins.

Glass and plastic go in the large blue bin. Paper and cardboard products go in the yellow bin. Aluminum cans go in the purple bin, but all other metals go in the red bin. Food waste should be put in the green bin.

Thank you for your cooperation,
Scherk Property Management

160. Where should you put cola bottles?

(A) In the blue bin
(B) In the yellow bin
(C) In the red bin
(D) In the green bin

161. Which of the following would you put in the yellow bin?

(A) Old shoes
(B) Food
(C) Magazines
(D) A broken TV

162. Which of the following can NOT be put in the green bin?

(A) Newspapers
(B) A leftover sandwich
(C) Orange peel
(D) Rice

GO ON TO THE NEXT PAGE

Ticket-King

Do you need tickets for the big event? We've got all your ticket needs covered!

We sell tickets for sporting events (football, hockey, baseball, even boxing), concerts (from Diana Krall to U2), and the theater.

Special this week only: 10% discount on all concert tickets. That's right, you can get your pass to the big Tragically Hip concert for just $45* after the discount. Buy yours today!

Visit us at www.ticket-king.com

*discount price does not include Ticket-King's additional 70% service charge

163. Where can you buy tickets?

(A) In a department store
(B) In the newspaper
(C) On the Internet
(D) In the shopping mall

164. For which event can you get a 10% discount?

(A) A Michael Jackson concert
(B) A hockey game
(C) A boxing match
(D) A play

165. How much does a ticket for the Tragically Hip concert normally cost?

(A) $40
(B) $45
(C) $50
(D) $55

JADE LION

Szechuan Style Chinese Restaurant
Dimsum, Peking Duck, Ginger Beef,
and all your mouth-watering favorites

Try our $9.99 lunch buffet Monday through Friday,
11:00 a.m. - 2:00 p.m.

Planning a party? No problem, book one of our many rooms.

56 West Sycamore Street (beside Eaton's Department Store)
Call 476-5593 for group reservations.
Call 476-5594 for takeout orders (pick-up or delivery)

Hours: Monday - Friday 11:00 a.m. - 10:00 p.m.
Saturday 12:00 p.m. - 11:00 p.m.

No MSG available upon request

166. What kind of food does the Jade Lion Restaurant serve?

(A) Korean food
(B) American food
(C) French food
(D) Chinese food

167. Which day is the restaurant NOT open?

(A) Monday
(B) Tuesday
(C) Saturday
(D) Sunday

168. What is the address of the restaurant?

(A) Jade Lion
(B) 11:00 a.m. - 9:00 p.m.
(C) 56 West Sycamore Street
(D) Beside Eaton's

GO ON TO THE NEXT PAGE

Questions 169 through 172 refer to the following schedule.

TOUR SCHEDULE

6:00 a.m.	• Get on bus in front of the Fairmont Hotel
7:15 a.m.	• Arrive in the city center
7:30 - 8:30	• Eat a traditional local breakfast prepared specially for our tour group by Fairmont's world-famous chefs
9:00 - 11:30	• Morning sightseeing includes stops at the Sarantis Art Museum, Herrera Street Craft Shops, and the Carolyn Botanical Gardens
12:00 - 1:00	• Buffet lunch at La Galleria de Niso
1:00 - 5:00	• Afternoon sightseeing includes more shopping and a tour of local clay-making workshops
5:15 p.m.	• Return to the bus
6:30 p.m.	• Arrive back at the Fairmont Hotel parking lot

169. How long is the bus ride to the city?

(A) One fifteen
(B) One hour and fifteen minutes
(C) Six o'clock
(D) Seven hours and fifteen minutes

170. Where will they eat breakfast?

(A) In the morning
(B) On the bus
(C) In the city
(D) At a workshop

171. When will they go sightseeing?

(A) In the morning and in the afternoon
(B) In the afternoon and in the evening
(C) In the morning and at night
(D) In the afternoon and at night

172. How long will this tour last?

(A) Two days
(B) Six hours
(C) 6:30 p.m.
(D) Twelve and a half hours

Questions 173 through 176 refer to the following letter.

April 10ᵗʰ,

Dear Harry,

Our new house is so nice. We have been living here for two months. We have such a big living room and dining room. Upstairs, there are three bedrooms and two bathrooms. Behind the house, we have trees, a swimming pool, and a garden for growing vegetables. In the front, we have a beautiful flower garden. I hope that you will come to visit someday.

Best wishes,
Jack

173. What is Jack writing about?

(A) His new house
(B) His family
(C) His dog
(D) His friend

174. What is upstairs?

(A) The living room
(B) The kitchen
(C) The swimming pool
(D) Three bedrooms

175. What is in front of the house?

(A) A vegetable garden
(B) A flower garden
(C) A swimming pool
(D) Three bathrooms

176. When did Jack move to his new house?

(A) In two months
(B) Recently
(C) In April
(D) In February

GO ON TO THE NEXT PAGE

Questions 177 through 180 refer to the following sign.

King's Department Store

Attention: Valued Customers

We're moving to our new, more luxurious downtown location next month! To avoid the high costs of moving our products, we're having a SPECIAL SALE!

5th Floor	All books and toys are 60% off.
4th Floor	Furniture, tools, and hardware at up to 70% off.
3rd Floor	Women's and girls' clothing at 40% off. (excluding swimwear)
2nd Floor	Men's and boys' clothing at 40% off. (excluding swimwear)
1st Floor	Up to 75% off all canned and dry goods in the supermarket.

177. Where can you buy a sofa?

(A) On the fourth floor
(B) On the fifth floor
(C) On the first floor
(D) On the second floor

178. Where should Peter and his father go to buy new clothes?

(A) To the fifth floor
(B) To the fourth floor
(C) To the third floor
(D) To the second floor

179. Where should Jack go to buy a new dictionary for English class?

(A) To the fifth floor
(B) To the fourth floor
(C) To the third floor
(D) To the second floor

180. Why is the store having a special sale?

(A) The floors were rearranged.
(B) The store will be relocating.
(C) The store rooms are full.
(D) It is closing down.

GO ON TO THE NEXT PAGE

Questions 181 through 185 refer to the following report and reply.

Report Card: MARY SMITH

Subject	Grade	Comments
English 11	B	Mary's writing continues to improve.
Math 11	A	Excellent work, Mary!
Science 11	C	Mary needs to work much harder.
Music 11	A+	It's a pleasure to have Mary in my class!
Art 11	B	Please practice more with oil paints.
History 11	B-	A large improvement. Keep working!
Phys. Ed. 11	A-	One of our top volleyball players!
Spanish 11	B+	Mary speaks quite well.

Parents: Please return the attached feedback form to show you have seen this report card.

Report card for Mary Smith

I confirm I have read the above report card.
Signed: S. R. Smith

Comments:
We are very happy to see Mary received an A for Math. She has really improved. Last time, she received a C. However, her English and Science results are disappointing. Her grades have dropped in these subjects. Do you think she needs extra science classes? We are worried that she won't get into a good university when she graduates high school. She has only one more year to prepare for graduation. Please advise us.

From
Mary's parents

181. In which class did Mary get the highest grade?

(A) English 11
(B) Math 11
(C) Science 11
(D) Music 11

182. In which class did Mary get the lowest grade?

(A) English 11
(B) Math 11
(C) Science 11
(D) Music 11

183. In which classes did Mary get the same grade?

(A) English 11 and Math 11
(B) Math 11 and Science 11
(C) Music 11 and Art 11
(D) English 11 and Art 11

184. What do Mary's parents think about her Math 11 grade?

(A) It could be better.
(B) It was better last year.
(C) It is much better than last year.
(D) It is terrible as always.

185. Why are Mary's parents worried?

(A) They think she will not be accepted by a good university.
(B) Mary doesn't want to go to a good university.
(C) They don't have enough money for a good university.
(D) They don't think Mary's teachers are very good.

GO ON TO THE NEXT PAGE

FOR SALE

A used living room set (sofa and two armchairs) made of the finest Corinthian leather. Only one year old and in perfect condition (no scratches or stains).

I'm selling them because I'm moving overseas and can't take them with me. $100 for the sofa and $50 for each chair, or $150 for the 3-piece set.

Call Michael Clemons at 555-3871 or send a message to sofa4sale@yahu.com.

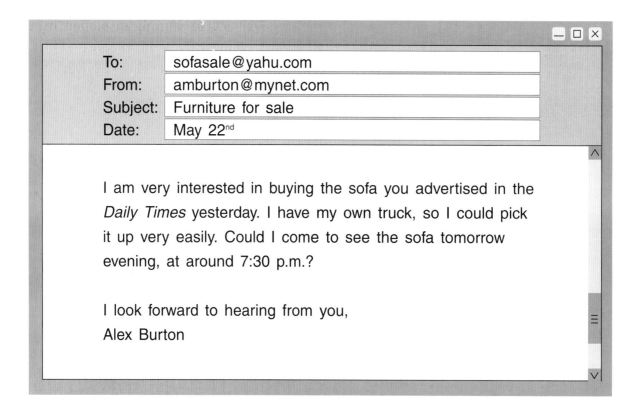

To:	sofasale@yahu.com
From:	amburton@mynet.com
Subject:	Furniture for sale
Date:	May 22nd

I am very interested in buying the sofa you advertised in the *Daily Times* yesterday. I have my own truck, so I could pick it up very easily. Could I come to see the sofa tomorrow evening, at around 7:30 p.m.?

I look forward to hearing from you,
Alex Burton

186. How much will it cost to buy the sofa and two chairs together?

(A) 50 dollars
(B) 100 dollars
(C) 150 dollars
(D) 200 dollars

187. How can you contact the seller?

(A) Only by telephone
(B) Only by email
(C) By email and telephone
(D) By telephone and fax

188. Where did Michael Clemons place this advertisement?

(A) On the Internet
(B) In a daily newspaper
(C) In a weekly magazine
(D) On TV

189. What does Alex Burton want to buy?

(A) All of the items
(B) One chair
(C) Two chairs
(D) Just the sofa

190. How will Alex Burton get his furniture home?

(A) Michael Clemons will deliver them.
(B) He will use his truck.
(C) He will use a delivery company.
(D) He can't take them home, so he decides to buy nothing.

GO ON TO THE NEXT PAGE

Questions 191 through 195 refer to the following emails.

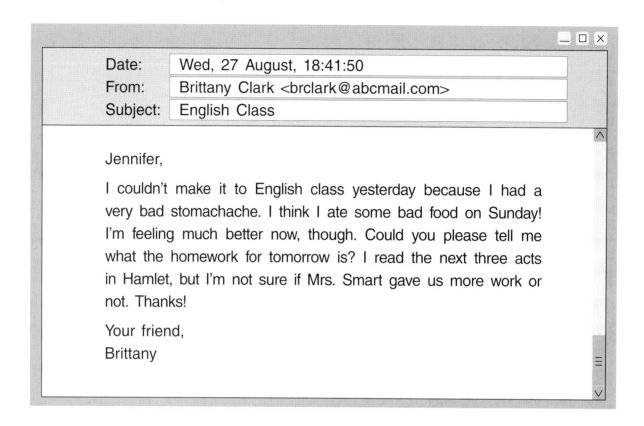

Date: Wed, 27 August, 18:41:50
From: Brittany Clark <brclark@abcmail.com>
Subject: English Class

Jennifer,

I couldn't make it to English class yesterday because I had a very bad stomachache. I think I ate some bad food on Sunday! I'm feeling much better now, though. Could you please tell me what the homework for tomorrow is? I read the next three acts in Hamlet, but I'm not sure if Mrs. Smart gave us more work or not. Thanks!

Your friend,
Brittany

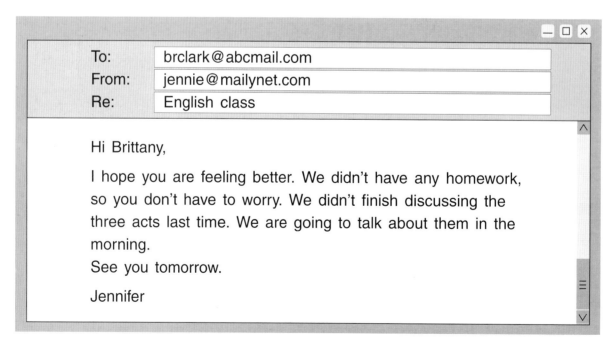

To: brclark@abcmail.com
From: jennie@mailynet.com
Re: English class

Hi Brittany,

I hope you are feeling better. We didn't have any homework, so you don't have to worry. We didn't finish discussing the three acts last time. We are going to talk about them in the morning.
See you tomorrow.

Jennifer

191. Why did Brittany miss English class yesterday?

(A) She was busy.
(B) She was sick.
(C) She forgot.
(D) She didn't do her homework.

192. What will Brittany and Jennifer do in English class tomorrow?

(A) Homework
(B) Read a play
(C) Discuss a play
(D) Write an essay

193. Who is Jennifer?

(A) A student in Brittany's English class
(B) Brittany's mother
(C) Brittany's sister
(D) Brittany's teacher

194. Who is Mrs. Smart?

(A) Brittany's mother
(B) Jennifer's mother
(C) Brittany and Jennifer's homeroom teacher
(D) Brittany and Jennifer's English teacher

195. Which of the following is NOT true?

(A) Brittany was absent yesterday.
(B) Jennifer attended the English class yesterday.
(C) There is a lot of homework for the next class.
(D) Brittany ate something bad.

GO ON TO THE NEXT PAGE ▶

HELP WANTED

Giorgio's World Famous Pizza House is now hiring people for the following positions:

- Cook (Two openings — experience required)
- Waiter (Four openings — experience preferred)
- Cashier (One opening — willing to train the right high school graduate)
- Dishwasher (One opening — must be physically fit)

Giorgio's offers good salaries and a very nice benefits package.

To apply, please bring your resume to the restaurant and ask to speak to the manager, Ms. Elissa Haggio.

Dear Ms. Haggio,

I am very interested in your job advertisement. I am a cook with over ten year's experience. I worked at Sandro's Spaghetti House for three years. I then worked at Pizza Amore for seven years. I am a very hardworking person and would like to work at Giorgio's. I often visit your restaurant and am always impressed by the food there.
I hope to hear from you.

Sincerely,

Mike Di Beni

196. Who is this advertisement for?

(A) People who like Italian food
(B) People named Giorgio
(C) People who have worked in restaurants before
(D) People who have never worked in restaurants before

197. How many people does the restaurant want to hire?

(A) Four
(B) Six
(C) Eight
(D) Ten

198. For which position is the restaurant not hiring?

(A) Manager
(B) Cook
(C) Dishwasher
(D) Waiter

199. How long has Mike Di Beni worked as a cook?

(A) Three years
(B) Seven years
(C) Ten years
(D) One week

200. Which of the following is NOT true?

(A) Mike Di Beni wants to work at Giorgio's Pizza House.
(B) Mike used to work at Sandro's Spaghetti House.
(C) Mike wants to be manager at Giorgio's Pizza House.
(D) Pay is good at Giorgio's Pizza House.

Support

Exercise 1

(A) He is yawning.
(B) They are crying.
(C) They are laughing.
(D) She is frowning.

Exercise 2

(A) They are kissing.
(B) They are clapping.
(C) She is acting on stage.
(D) She is nodding her head.

Part 1

1. (A) This is a small house.
(B) This is a big house.
(C) This is a doghouse.
(D) This is a greenhouse.

2. (A) There are boats on the water.
(B) There are boats at the park.
(C) There are boats at the beach.
(D) There is a boat in the museum.

3. (A) The men are working.
(B) The men are playing.
(C) The men are clapping.
(D) The men are laughing.

4. (A) The woman is wearing a scarf.
(B) The woman is wearing a hat.
(C) The man is wearing a tie.
(D) The man is wearing a hat.

5. (A) The tree is in front of the woman.
(B) The telephone is behind the woman.
(C) The keyboard is under the desk.
(D) The computer is next to the woman.

Part 2

1. Where is he going?

(A) She's going to the store.
(B) I'm going to the store.
(C) He's going to the store.

2. Phew! It's hot in here!

(A) I'll turn on the fan.
(B) I'll turn on the heat.
(C) I'll turn on the lights.

3. What are you watching?

(A) You're watching a movie.
(B) I'm watching a movie.
(C) I'll watch a movie.

4. How did you do that?

(A) I did it.
(B) It's easy. I'll show you.
(C) No, you didn't.

5. When do you wake up?

(A) Since 7:00.
(B) I'm waking up.
(C) Usually at 8:00.

Part 3

Questions 1 through 3 refer to the following conversation.

M: Mary, who's that woman over there with short hair?
W: The woman making photocopies?
M: Right. Is she new here?
W: Yes. She is the new receptionist.

Questions 4 through 6 refer to the following conversation.

W: I have a terrible headache.
M: Well, why don't you turn on the lights?
W: Wow, that's much better.
M: You are going to damage your eyes. My wife's sister had the same problem.

Part 4

Questions 1 through 3 refer to the following talk.

M: I usually ride my bicycle to work. It's much faster than taking the bus because I can take a shortcut through the park. It takes about twenty minutes in total. The subway is even slower because it is a fifteen-minute walk from my house to the subway station. Then the subway ride is another twenty minutes. In the winter, though, I have to take the bus because of the weather.

Questions 4 through 6 refer to the following talk.

W: I'm a wedding planner. My job brings me a lot of pleasure. Today is an amazing day. I am planning my sister's wedding. She will wear a beautiful white dress. I also get to wear a lovely dress. After the wedding, all the guests will have a nice dinner and will dance for hours. In the evening my sister and her new husband will cut a cake that I designed. I hope they like it a lot.

Exercise 1

(A) He is shopping.
(B) He is paying the bill.
(C) He is trying on shoes.
(D) She is selling fruit.

Exercise 2

(A) She is returning a video.
(B) He is lending her some money.
(C) She is counting money.
(D) They are shaking hands.

Part 1

1. (A) He is selling his car.
   (B) He is trying on the golf clubs.
   (C) He is counting the cars.
   (D) He is holding the golf clubs.

2. (A) They are paying the dog.
   (B) They are washing the dog.
   (C) They are cleaning the cat.
   (D) They are shaking their pet.

3. (A) The woman is sitting on a chair.
   (B) The woman is selling a magazine.
   (C) The woman is lending the magazine.
   (D) The woman is in a hotel room.

4. (A) The man is clapping his hands.
   (B) The man is in a pool.
   (C) The man is playing basketball.
   (D) The man is borrowing a ball.

5. (A) The man is jogging.
   (B) The man is taking a picture.
   (C) The man is painting.
   (D) The man is skating.

Part 2

1. Who were you talking to?

   (A) To the store.
   (B) To buy some ice cream.
   (C) To a friend.

2. Why did you leave early?

   (A) I was tired.
   (B) She is more tired.
   (C) You are tired.

3. When is your brother's birthday?

   (A) Last year.
   (B) Next Tuesday.
   (C) On time.

4. I'm so tired.

   (A) I should take a nap.
   (B) You should take a nap.
   (C) He took a nap.

5. Is the window open?

   (A) No, it doesn't.
   (B) Yes, it does.
   (C) No, it isn't.

Part 3

<u>Questions 1 through 3</u> refer to the following conversation.

W: Excuse me, haven't we met before?
M: Yes, I used to work at Evan's Department Store.
W: That's right. You sold shoes there.
M: Yes, but now I have my own store.

<u>Questions 4 through 6</u> refer to the following conversation.

M: I'm back. Sorry I'm late.
W: What took you so long? You missed an appointment with Eric.
M: I know, but the traffic was really bad.
W: Well, he wants you to call him. He seemed a little angry.

Part 4

<u>Questions 1 through 3</u> refer to the following announcement.

W: Attention, please. We would like to remind you that next Monday at nine o'clock, we will be having our yearly staff picnic. All staff and their families are invited to attend. Plenty of food and drink will be provided for everyone, and we will be having our famous barbecue. We will also have our annual fun and games. Prizes include a new DVD player and a holiday.

<u>Questions 4 through 6</u> refer to the following talk.

M: After university, I want to be a doctor. Doctors have very important jobs. When I was younger, my mom was very sick. She stayed in the hospital for one month. I was so happy when she returned home. It really made me want to be a doctor so that I could help sick people, too. It is hard work to become a doctor, but I'm going to study hard.

Exercise 1

   (A) She is riding a bike.
   (B) She is swimming.
   (C) The man is stretching.
   (D) She is playing tennis.

Exercise 2

   (A) They are dancing.
   (B) They are making a sand castle.
   (C) She is kicking the ball.
   (D) He is rowing the boat.

Part 1

1. (A) This is a meeting room.
   (B) This is a church.
   (C) This is a garden.
   (D) This is a hospital.

2. (A) They have a kite.
   (B) They have a balloon.
   (C) They have an airplane.
   (D) They have a book.

3. (A) The girl is stretching.
   (B) The girl is next to the dog.
   (C) The girl is dancing.
   (D) The girl is under the dog.

4. (A) The man is singing.
   (B) The man is dancing.
   (C) The man is angry.
   (D) The man is rowing.

5. (A) The person is writing.
   (B) The person is cutting.
   (C) The person is painting.
   (D) The person is laughing.

Part 2

1. How have you been lately?

   (A) I'm sorry, I'm late.
   (B) Great.
   (C) Two hours.

2. Did you enjoy shopping?

   (A) I like food.
   (B) It was too expensive.
   (C) We'll have a great party.

3. When did the show start?

   (A) I don't have time right now.
   (B) Twenty minutes ago.
   (C) In a couple of hours.

4. What do you like to do in your free time?

   (A) Go shopping.
   (B) I'm very busy now.
   (C) You have to finish it by Friday.

5. How did you find the movie?

   (A) It was around the corner.
   (B) It was very scary.
   (C) We might be late for the movie.

Part 3

Questions 1 through 3 refer to the following conversation.

M: Are we going to buy the green curtains or the yellow curtains for the main conference room?

W: The manager decided to go for green. I think it's a good choice.

M: Yes, I hope it will help reduce stress during meetings.

Questions 4 through 6 refer to the following conversation.

M: What's the matter?

W: I can't find my glasses.

M: They are probably on your desk.

W: No. Ah, yes! I remember leaving them in my car.

Part 4

Questions 1 through 3 refer to the following announcement.

W: Due to problems with the lighting, the concert has to be postponed until Friday the 22ⁿᵈ. The concert will also be moved from hall A to the larger hall C. A bigger venue means a further five hundred tickets will now be available, twice the original number. Because of the extra tickets, tickets will now be priced at the lower cost of twenty dollars.

Questions 4 through 6 refer to the following talk.

M: This year at university, I am studying three languages. English is the most difficult. French and Spanish are both quite easy. I have lots of chances to practice Spanish because I live with my Mexican friend. I am getting used to speaking Spanish outside of class.

Exercise 1

(A) They are building a house.
(B) He is working on a computer.
(C) He is designing a building.
(D) She is wrapping a gift.

Exercise 2

(A) He is delivering some flowers.
(B) She is typing.
(C) She is serving drinks.
(D) He is measuring the table.

Part 1

1. (A) The boy is looking at the girl.
(B) They are looking at the book.
(C) The book is on the chair.
(D) The girl is looking at the teacher.

2. (A) The birds are on the boat.
(B) The birds are flying.
(C) The birds are in the water.
(D) The birds are in a tree.

3. (A) The men are skiing.
(B) The men are skating.
(C) The men are swimming.
(D) The men are jogging.

4. (A) The man is holding a book.
(B) The man is sitting on the sofa.
(C) The man is reading a newspaper.
(D) The man is at the bus stop.

5. (A) The people are standing.
(B) The people are walking.
(C) The people are running.
(D) The people are jumping.

Part 2

1. What time does the movie start?

(A) At three thirty.
(B) It's a good movie.
(C) It's three o'clock.

2. How old are you?

(A) I'm fine, thank you.
(B) I'm fifteen.
(C) I feel sick.

3. Do you like chocolate ice cream?

(A) No, I can't.
(B) Yes, I do.
(C) Yes, I can.

4. Where did she go?

(A) Yes, she did.
(B) To the supermarket.
(C) She's going now.

5. Why did you close the window?

(A) The window is closed.
(B) It's a window.
(C) Because it's cold.

Part 3

Questions 1 through 3 refer to the following conversation.

M: Can I use your computer?
W: No. It's broken.
M: What's wrong with it?
W: I can't save documents, and I have an important presentation tomorrow!

Questions 4 through 6 refer to the following conversation.

M: One ticket from New York to Los Angeles, please.
W: With Express Air, that is two hundred and fifty dollars.
M: That's too expensive. Do you have anything cheaper?
W: The other airlines are asking the same price.

Part 4

Questions 1 through 3 refer to the following announcement.

W: Attention all passengers on flight KL162 from Spain to Ireland. This flight has been delayed due to bad weather. The flight will now be leaving at 7:15 p.m., from gate 22A. We apologize for any inconvenience.

Questions 4 through 6 refer to the following talk.

M: If you look to your right, you can see the biggest black bear we have here at Funland. His name is King. He weighs over 500 pounds. He is one of the ten bears we have at Funland. He has been at Funland for over fifteen years.

Exercise 1

(A) She is calling someone.
(B) She is saying goodbye.
(C) She is shouting.
(D) They are chatting.

Exercise 2

(A) She is speaking to the class.
(B) He is talking on the phone.
(C) He is whispering to his friend.
(D) She is yelling at the dog.

Part 1

1. (A) They are singing.
   (B) They are crying.
   (C) They are dancing.
   (D) They are fighting.

2. (A) The cow is walking on the road.
   (B) The cow is eating the grass.
   (C) The cow is standing in the water.
   (D) The cow is on the truck.

3. (A) The couple is sleeping.
   (B) The couple is camping.
   (C) The couple is hiking.
   (D) The couple is smoking.

4. (A) The food is under the table.
   (B) The food is on the table.
   (C) The food is next to the table.
   (D) The food is in the sink.

5. (A) These are gifts.
   (B) These are birthdays.
   (C) These are Christmases.
   (D) These are squares.

Part 2

1. When are you leaving?

   (A) I live in New York.
   (B) She lives with me.
   (C) I'm leaving at eight o'clock.

2. Let's get some pizza!

   (A) How do you like pizza?
   (B) That's a good idea!
   (C) Pizza comes from Italy.

3. The test was very difficult.

   (A) I agree.
   (B) Yes, it has.
   (C) We took a test.

4. Is Jennifer at home?

   (A) No, she hasn't.
   (B) Yes, she did.
   (C) No, she isn't.

5. What does she do?

   (A) He's watching TV.
   (B) She does it every day.
   (C) She's a doctor.

Part 3

Questions 1 through 3 refer to the following conversation.

W: Excuse me, where's the post office?
M: It's next to the library.
W: Is it far from here? I need to be in the city center in an hour.
M: No. It takes five to ten minutes on foot.

Questions 4 through 6 refer to the following conversation.

W: Where are you going?
M: To the store to buy some bread and milk.
W: Could you get some eggs too?
M: Sure. I'll bring back a box.

Part 4

Questions 1 through 3 refer to the following talk.

M: I'm lucky because I really like my job. It doesn't feel like work. I've been singing with my cousin in bars and restaurants for more than fifteen years. I really enjoy it, but I would love to sing in the theater some day. That is my dream.

Questions 4 through 6 refer to the following advertisement.

W: Is your cell phone old? Do all your friends have new camera phones? If you want one, too, you should come down to Phonetown this weekend. We are selling all cell phones at half-price. Come down to Phonetown. You would be crazy to miss this sale!

Exercise 1

(A) She is raising her hand.
(B) He is pointing to the sign.
(C) She is waving.
(D) He is writing on the board.

Exercise 2

(A) They are hugging.
(B) He is helping the child.
(C) He is showing her the map.
(D) She is cheering for the team.

Part 1

1. (A) The teddy bear is in the box.
   (B) The teddy bear is on the box.
   (C) The teddy bear is under the box.
   (D) The teddy bear is next to the box.

2. (A) They are having a car race.
   (B) They are having curry and rice.
   (C) They are holding two cars.
   (D) They are building cars.

3. (A) These are two dolls.
   (B) These are two bees.
   (C) These are two parrots.
   (D) These are two plates.

4. (A) The man is looking at the list.
   (B) The man is carrying a box.
   (C) The man is standing behind the shelf.
   (D) The man is writing a letter.

5. (A) The woman is playing basketball.
   (B) The woman is playing soccer.
   (C) The woman is playing golf.
   (D) The woman is playing volleyball.

Part 2

1. When is your sister's birthday?

   (A) Next Tuesday.
   (B) Tuesday is the sixth.
   (C) She's six years old.

2. Have you seen that movie?

   (A) I like movies.
   (B) Not yet.
   (C) That's my favorite actor.

3. Where is he from?

   (A) He's coming.
   (B) He's from Chicago.
   (C) He'll come tomorrow.

4. Do you like my new shoes?

   (A) Yes, they're very nice.
   (B) I like shoes.
   (C) I have new shoes.

5. I'm really hungry.

   (A) Here, have some cookies.
   (B) I don't know.
   (C) Look at this cookie.

Part 3

Questions 1 through 3 refer to the following conversation

W: Time Bookstore. How may I help you?
M: Hello. Could you tell me your opening hours?
W: We are open from nine to five Monday through Friday, and from ten to six on Saturdays. We are closed on Sundays.
M: I see. Thank you for your help.

Questions 4 through 6 refer to the following conversation

M: Have you seen my gloves? I can't find them.
W: Are they the brown ones that your mother gave you for Christmas?
M: No, the blue ones that she gave me for my birthday.
W: Umm, well, I have no idea where they are.

Part 4

Questions 1 through 3 refer to the following talk.

W: When I first moved to America, I felt quite lonely. I didn't have any friends, and I didn't know any fun places to go to. Also, I didn't like the food. Now, I have lots of friends and lots of things to do.

Questions 4 through 6 refer to the following talk.

M: I started taking Taekwondo lessons last year. It was my friend Sam who told me about Taekwondo. Now, I feel much stronger and I can move much faster. Next year, I want to get my black belt like Sam!

Exercise 1

(A) The cat is eating.
(B) He is having dinner.
(C) He is chewing gum.
(D) He is feeding the fish.

Exercise 2

(A) He is cooking.
(B) She is pouring some tea.
(C) She is giving him a cake.
(D) He is bringing her some tea.

Part 1

1. (A) The girls are crying.
(B) The girls are laughing.
(C) The girls are frowning.
(D) The girls are smiling.

2. (A) This is a father and two daughters.
(B) This is a husband and wife.
(C) This is a brother and sister.
(D) This is a mother and two sons.

3. (A) This is a swimming pool.
(B) This is a health club.
(C) This is a beach.
(D) This is a mountain.

4. (A) These are trees.
(B) These are flowers.
(C) These are animals.
(D) These are fruit.

5. (A) They are in a hotel.
(B) They are in a bank.
(C) They are in a hospital.
(D) They are in a park.

Part 2

1. What's today's date?

(A) It's Tuesday.
(B) It's the twentieth.
(C) Yesterday.

2. Did you have a good time?

(A) Yes, you did.
(B) Yes, we did.
(C) Yes, he did.

3. Would you like something to drink?

(A) You're welcome.
(B) I'm hungry.
(C) No, thank you.

4. How did you get here?

(A) I took the bus.
(B) I take the bus.
(C) I'll take the bus.

5. When does your class finish?

(A) At four o'clock.
(B) It's four o'clock.
(C) Four hours.

Part 3

Questions 1 through 3 refer to the following conversation.

M: Which one is Mary? I heard that she is the new manager.
W: She's the one wearing the red dress and black jacket. She has long black hair.
M: Oh, that's Mary. I expected her to be older.
W: Well, she's older than she looks, you know.

Questions 4 through 6 refer to the following conversation.

W: What should I bring to the picnic tomorrow? Do I need to bring any food?
M: You could bring some sandwiches, or a few cookies to share. Something that is easy to eat with your fingers.
W: Oh, that's a good idea. I'll bring some brownies.
M: Great. See you at eleven in the morning.

Part 4

Questions 1 through 3 refer to the following talk.

M: This is my friend Pablo from Spain. He came here six months ago. He is here studying Korean and Economics at Seoul National University. He speaks Korean very well, and he really enjoys Korean food. He will be going back to Madrid next February.

Questions 4 through 6 refer to the following announcement.

W: Could the owner of a green and red Daesung Santa Lucia, registration number ST 4571 please come to the parking lot immediately. Your car is blocking the entrance. A delivery truck is unable to enter and this is causing a traffic jam in the street outside the store.

Exercise 1

(A) They are loading bags into the car.
(B) The rabbit is hopping.
(C) The frog is jumping.
(D) The dog is chasing the cat.

Exercise 2

(A) He is fixing the car.
(B) The bird is flying.
(C) The dog is playing with the ball.
(D) They are marching in a parade.

Part 1

1. (A) This is a party.
   (B) This is a meeting.
   (C) This is a concert.
   (D) This is a parade.

2. (A) The man is next to the bicycle.
   (B) The man is behind the bicycle.
   (C) The man is in the bicycle.
   (D) The man is on the bicycle.

3. (A) The man is standing on the car.
   (B) The man is standing in the car.
   (C) The man is standing next to the car.
   (D) The man is standing under the car.

4. (A) The horse is standing.
   (B) The horse is walking.
   (C) The horse is running.
   (D) The horse is jumping.

5. (A) They are swimming.
   (B) They are jogging.
   (C) They are playing basketball.
   (D) They are playing volleyball.

Part 2

1. Could you lend me some money?

   (A) That's a great idea.
   (B) I have to go shopping.
   (C) I'm sorry, I'm broke.

2. Is it OK if I turn on the heater?

   (A) Sure, go ahead.
   (B) It's a nice day.
   (C) Yes, it's quite hot in here.

3. What time shall we meet?

   (A) I'm glad that you came.
   (B) How about 2 p.m. tomorrow?
   (C) Sorry, I'm busy at the moment.

4. How can I help you, sir?

   (A) I'm fine, thank you.
   (B) I'm interested in buying a T-shirt.
   (C) No way.

5. Excuse me. Where's the nearest station?

   (A) It's over there.
   (B) You're welcome.
   (C) Let's go.

Part 3

Questions 1 through 3 refer to the following conversation.

W: So, when do you have to leave? Aren't you catching a bus to New York?
M: Pretty soon. But I'm actually taking a train to New Jersey first, then catching a bus. The train leaves in ten minutes.
W: Then we'd better hurry up. You don't want to miss your train.
M: It's OK. I have everything ready to go.

Questions 4 through 6 refer to the following conversation.

M: Hello, I'm Peter, your new neighbor. My wife and I just moved in next door.
W: Nice to meet you, I'm Sara. I think I saw your children playing in the street earlier.
M: Yes, we have a son and a daughter. They are twins.

Part 4

Questions 1 through 3 refer to the following advertisement.

M: Are you interested in learning Korean? If so, come to our free classes at Hondo English Institute. Here, learning is fun. Students learn Korean with people from many different countries. Classes begin at twelve o'clock on Saturdays and two o'clock on Sundays.

Questions 4 through 6 refer to the following talk.

W: I have been working at the zoo for over twenty years now. Every day, I have to feed the elephants and make sure that they have enough water. On my break, I like to walk around the zoo and look at the other animals. The hippo is my second favorite animal, after the elephant.

Exercise 1

(A) He is combing his hair.
(B) She is cutting a cake.
(C) He is cleaning a lamp.
(D) He is washing the dishes.

Exercise 2

(A) He is checking the mailbox.
(B) He is polishing his shoes.
(C) He is sweeping.
(D) She is folding the clothes.

Part 1

1. (A) The boy is playing a violin.
   (B) The boy is playing a piano.
   (C) The boy is playing with a friend.
   (D) The boy is playing in the yard.

2. (A) The couple is dressed for the beach.
   (B) The couple is dressed for skiing.
   (C) The couple is dressed for a party.
   (D) The couple is dressed for cleaning.

3. (A) The man is playing.
   (B) The man is working.
   (C) The man is eating.
   (D) The man is resting.

4. (A) They are looking at the table.
   (B) They are looking at the glasses.
   (C) They are looking at each other.
   (D) They are looking at the woman.

5. (A) The couple is in the city.
   (B) The couple is at the beach.
   (C) The couple is at home.
   (D) The couple is in the mountains.

Part 2

1. Your shoes look so nice.

   (A) They're mine.
   (B) I have shoes.
   (C) I just polished them.

2. How many people are there?

   (A) Fewer than last year.
   (B) More as today.
   (C) There are people.

3. This floor is so dirty.

   (A) I'm clapping.
   (B) Wait. I'll sweep it.
   (C) I'm already clean.

4. Flying is too expensive.

   (A) But it's faster than driving.
   (B) It's cheaper than taking an airplane.
   (C) This coffee is cheap.

5. When is the concert?

   (A) At downtown.
   (B) On Sunday.
   (C) In Tuesday.

Part 3

Questions 1 through 3 refer to the following conversation.

M: Are you drinking coffee again? How much coffee do you drink?
W: I'm not sure, but at least five cups a day.
M: That's too much. You should cut down.
W: But coffee helps me concentrate on my work!

Questions 4 through 6 refer to the following conversation.

W: Did you go to Sarah's party last night? It was great.
M: Yes, but I didn't see you there. What time did you leave?
W: I went home about 10 p.m.
M: Oh, you left before I arrived. I was there much later than you.

Part 4

Questions 1 through 3 refer to the following talk.

M: My schedule is as busy as my friends' schedules. Usually, I wake up at 7:00. I get on a bus at 8:00 and arrive at work at 9:00. After I get off work, at about 6:00, I go shopping or walk through the park with my wife. Sometimes, when I want a quiet evening, I just stay at home and watch TV.

Questions 4 through 6 refer to the following advertisement.

W: Hop on down to Bunny Motors for our huge sales event! We have the fastest and most expensive cars on the market, but you can now save up to 50% on the purchase of a new automobile. Want to seem richer and be smarter than all your neighbors? Then hop on down to Bunny Motors today!

Exercise 1

(A) She is painting a picture.
(B) He is watching television.
(C) They are singing.
(D) She is playing the guitar.

Exercise 2

(A) She is taking a bath.
(B) He is reading a book.
(C) She is relaxing by the pool.
(D) She is lying in the sun.

Part 1

1. (A) They are standing on the grass.
   (B) They are running on the grass.
   (C) They are lying on the grass.
   (D) They are sleeping on the grass.

2. (A) The man is holding a brush.
   (B) The man is holding a painting.
   (C) The man is holding a hat.
   (D) The man is holding a glass.

3. (A) This is a computer.
   (B) This is a phone.
   (C) This is a fax machine.
   (D) This is a calculator.

4. (A) These are boxes.
   (B) These are dice.
   (C) These are squares.
   (D) These are ice cubes.

5. (A) The man is sitting.
   (B) The man is standing.
   (C) The man is sleeping.
   (D) The man is swimming.

Part 2

1. How often does he play tennis?

   (A) He played tennis yesterday.
   (B) He's going to play tennis.
   (C) He plays tennis every day.

2. When did you see her?

   (A) I saw her last night.
   (B) I saw her with John.
   (C) I'll see her yesterday.

3. What's on TV tonight?

   (A) There's a movie at eight o'clock.
   (B) The book is on the TV.
   (C) It's under the TV.

4. How old is your car?

   (A) I'm five years old.
   (B) It's five years old.
   (C) It's ten years.

5. Do you have any pets?

   (A) Yes, I have a bicycle.
   (B) Yes, I have a brother.
   (C) Yes, I have a rabbit.

Part 3

Questions 1 through 3 refer to the following conversation.

M: Excuse me, is there a bookstore near here?
W: Yes. Go straight for one block, then turn left. It's right next to the bank.
M: Thank you.
W: No problem. They have a good selection, so you should find the book you need.

Questions 4 through 6 refer to the following conversation.

W: Are you going to the supermarket?
M: Yes. Do you need anything?
W: Could you pick me up some nice soap? I want to take a relaxing bath tonight.
M: Maybe you should come, too. I might buy the wrong kind.

Part 4

Questions 1 through 3 refer to the following talk.

M: I have been studying judo for over ten years. During my last competition, one opponent pulled my shoulder out of its socket. Despite the pain, I was able to throw my opponent to the ground because I really didn't want to lose. After, the referee raised my hand in victory.

Questions 4 through 6 refer to the following talk.

W: Over the past few years, I've had many jobs in the service industry. My duties included watering plants, sweeping floors, and serving customers in a restaurant. So, even though I look very young, I have a lot of experience. If you choose to hire me, I can be available to start work as soon as tomorrow morning.

Exercise 1

(A) The cat is hiding under the chair.
(B) She is standing in line.
(C) She is waiting for a bus.
(D) She is getting up.

Exercise 2

(A) He is resting in bed.
(B) He is wearing a scarf.
(C) They are listening to the bird.
(D) She is looking at the boat.

Part 1

1. (A) The man is holding a hat.
   (B) The man is holding a glove.
   (C) The man is holding a rabbit.
   (D) The man is holding a necktie.

2. (A) People are at a supermarket.
   (B) People are at a café.
   (C) People are at the beach.
   (D) People are at the post office.

3. (A) The man is holding a turtle.
   (B) The man is holding a snake.
   (C) The man is holding a fish.
   (D) The man is holding a camera.

4. (A) The beach is near the city.
   (B) The beach is far away from the city.
   (C) The beach looks very cold.
   (D) The beach is closed.

5. (A) There are umbrellas over the tables.
   (B) There are people wearing umbrellas.
   (C) There are no empty chairs at the table.
   (D) There are children in the pool.

Part 2

1. How was the movie?

   (A) It's a movie.
   (B) It was interesting.
   (C) It will be fun.

2. What's in your bag?

   (A) Nothing special.
   (B) I have a bag.
   (C) This is my bag.

3. Have you finished your homework?

   (A) Almost.
   (B) I am home.
   (C) Your homework is finished.

4. When does summer vacation start?

   (A) It starts next week.
   (B) It started next week.
   (C) I like vacations.

5. How long have you lived here?

   (A) For ten years.
   (B) Yesterday.
   (C) Until tomorrow.

Part 3

Questions 1 through 3 refer to the following conversation.

W: How much does an envelope cost?
M: The large ones are 75 cents each, but the smaller ones are 50 cents each. We also have three extra large sizes available.
W: Will you give a discount if I buy in bulk?
M: Yes, you can get 10% off if you buy at least 100.

Questions 4 through 6 refer to the following conversation.

M: May I help you, madam?
W: I'm trying to work out which train to take to Midland.
M: There's an express train in 45 minutes, or a local train leaving in ten minutes.
W: The local train takes much longer, but it is much cheaper. I guess I can catch up on some reading.

Part 4

Questions 1 through 3 refer to the following advertisement.

M: Do you find it difficult to relax? Are you always stressed? If so, the answer to your problem is yoga. Yoga can help your body relax and give you a lot more energy. Contact the Rama Yoga Center at 311-4265 for more information.

Questions 4 through 6 refer to the following talk.

W: Two years ago, I went on vacation to Canada. I really enjoyed it. I went for walks in the mountains by myself. Then, I would meet my friends and we would have dinner together. I would love to go back on another vacation!

Exercise 1

(A) He is watering the garden.
(B) She is climbing a tree.
(C) They are walking in the park.
(D) She is throwing the ball.

Exercise 2

(A) They are gathering flowers.
(B) He is digging in the garden.
(C) She is picking a flower.
(D) He is parking the car.

Part 1

1. (A) This is a computer.
(B) This is a table.
(C) This is a mouse.
(D) This is a cat.

2. (A) The girl is eating.
(B) The girl is smiling.
(C) The girl is frowning.
(D) The girl is parking.

3. (A) This is a town.
(B) This is a city.
(C) This is a garden.
(D) This is a farm.

4. (A) These are grapes.
(B) These are peaches.
(C) These are strawberries.
(D) These are melons.

5. (A) The woman is in the bathroom.
(B) The woman is in the office.
(C) The woman is in the park.
(D) The woman is in the garage.

Part 2

1. Do you know Mary?

(A) Yes, we've met before.
(B) No, she isn't.
(C) She looks like Mary.

2. Can you play the piano?

(A) Only a little bit.
(B) I can't afford one.
(C) I like piano music.

3. What time is it?

(A) Of six o'clock.
(B) It's six o'clock.
(C) After six hours.

4. This cake is delicious!

(A) We have some cake.
(B) Cake has a lot of sugar.
(C) Thank you.

5. Do you like chocolate?

(A) This is chocolate.
(B) Of course.
(C) Chocolate comes from Mexico.

Part 3

Questions 1 through 3 refer to the following conversation.

W: The traffic is so busy here.
M: Yes, I hate trying to park downtown. It always takes so long to find a space.
W: Look, there's a spot over there. Let's take it.
M: At last. I can't believe it took us 15 minutes to park. We wasted so much time.

Questions 4 through 6 refer to the following conversation.

M: Hi Jane. Have you been waiting long?
W: Yes, I arrived an hour ago. Why were you so late?
M: Why did you come so early? I thought we agreed to meet at 3:30?
W: No, we said 2:30. You got it wrong yet again.

Part 4

Questions 1 through 3 refer to the following talk.

M: In the event of a fire, please follow these directions. Stand up and walk towards the nearest exit. Do not run, and do not try to gather your things. When outside, wait for your teacher on the football field. Next week we will have the first of our two annual fire drills. Thank you.

Questions 4 through 6 refer to the following talk.

W: Please listen carefully to the instructions. When you hear the bell, please turn over your paper and begin the test. Write your name and class number on the first page. There are three parts to the test. You have one hour to complete each part.

Part 1

1. (A) There is one hand.
(B) This is a keyboard.
(C) This is a board.
(D) There are two computers.

2. (A) The people are swimming.
(B) The people are standing.
(C) The people are watching a show.
(D) The people are watching TV.

3. (A) This is a boat.
(B) This is a market.
(C) This is a truck.
(D) This is a fish.

4. (A) The women are singing.
(B) The women are sitting.
(C) The women are dancing.
(D) The women are chatting.

5. (A) The woman is talking on the phone.
(B) The woman is crying.
(C) The woman is frowning.
(D) The woman is laughing.

6. (A) The car is for sale.
(B) The car is on top of the building.
(C) The car is inside the house.
(D) The car is in front of the house.

7. (A) The people are reading the menu.
(B) They have no menus.
(C) The waiter is giving them a menu.
(D) They're sharing one menu.

8. (A) People are in the swimming pool.
(B) People are on the beach.
(C) People are at the tennis courts.
(D) People are in the restaurant.

9. (A) The man is sleeping on the table.
(B) The man is sitting next to the table.
(C) The man is drinking from the glass.
(D) The man is holding a bottle.

10. (A) The man is riding a jet ski.
(B) The man is jumping in the water.
(C) The man is swimming fast.
(D) The man is flying over the water.

Part 2

11. The radio is too loud!
(A) I'm sorry, I'll turn it off.
(B) Thank you very much!
(C) You're welcome.

12. What's your phone number?
(A) I'm twelve years old.
(B) At six o'clock.
(C) 555-3481.

13. Would you like to dance?
(A) Yes, I'd like that.
(B) Yes, I can.
(C) Yes, you like to dance.

14. What time did you wake up this morning?
(A) It's seven o'clock.
(B) Seven hours.
(C) At seven o'clock.

15. Are you finished with that newspaper?
(A) Yes, you're welcome.
(B) No, not yet.
(C) No, thank you.

16. Do you like classical music?
(A) Yes, I can.
(B) Yes, I am.
(C) Yes, I do.

17. Thank you very much for your help.
(A) You're welcome.
(B) Here you are.
(C) No, thanks.

18. Excuse me, do you sell umbrellas?
(A) No, we haven't.
(B) No, we don't.
(C) No, we aren't.

19. Where is the restaurant?
(A) It's next to the bank.
(B) It's next to the restaurant.
(C) Yes, here it is.

20. Do you want to go swimming?

    (A) You want to go swimming.

    (B) Yes, she wants to go swimming.

    (C) No, it's too cold.

21. Where are they going?

    (A) We're going downtown.

    (B) They're going downtown.

    (C) You're going downtown.

22. What did you get for your birthday?

    (A) I got a bicycle.

    (B) I have a bicycle.

    (C) I'm riding a bicycle.

23. Did you go to Sarah's party last night?

    (A) Yes, I was.

    (B) No, I didn't.

    (C) No, I wasn't.

24. Would you mind closing the door?

    (A) You're welcome.

    (B) Never mind.

    (C) Not at all.

25. What's wrong with Peter?

    (A) He's got a cold.

    (B) He got an A on the test.

    (C) He's with Peter.

26. How was the test?

    (A) It was easy.

    (B) They were easy.

    (C) He was easy.

27. That cake looks really delicious.

    (A) Would you like some pieces?

    (B) Would you like a piece?

    (C) Do you like a piece?

28. Is that a new jacket?

    (A) Yes, I did it yesterday.

    (B) Yes, I bought it yesterday.

    (C) Yes, I had it yesterday.

29. I'm sorry that I'm so late.

    (A) You're welcome.

    (B) Yes, please.

    (C) No problem.

30. This book is really interesting.

    (A) I agree.

    (B) I'm a book.

    (C) I have an interest.

31. Do you know where my book is?

    (A) A math book.

    (B) Yes, it's on the sofa.

    (C) The library is open.

32. Where did you go on Saturday?

    (A) They went to the movies.

    (B) I went to a party.

    (C) I enjoyed the party.

33. Where is that new restaurant?

    (A) It's downtown.

    (B) It's a new restaurant.

    (C) I went to it yesterday.

34. Which bus do I take to the theater?

    (A) You take it from here.

    (B) The bus will be here soon.

    (C) You take the number ten.

35. Could you please buy some milk at the store?

    (A) Sure.

    (B) I'm going to the store.

    (C) I like milk.

36. Who are you going on vacation with?

    (A) I'm going to France.

    (B) It's very warm there.

    (C) I'm going with my family.

37. When do you go to the gym?

    (A) I finish work at six.

    (B) I usually go after work.

    (C) The gym is usually very busy.

38. What will you buy with the money?

    (A) I bought a new car.

    (B) I buy clothes.

    (C) I will buy a new cell phone.

39. Where will you be working in your new job?

    (A) I start tomorrow.

    (B) I will be working at the bank.

    (C) I work with my uncle.

40. Why didn't you eat your dinner?

    (A) I am hungry.

    (B) I didn't have time.

    (C) Steak, I think.

Part 3

Questions 41 through 43 refer to this conversation.

M: When do you leave for the big conference?

W: Tomorrow morning. It's in New York.

M: How long will you stay there?

W: Just two nights. I'll be back on Friday evening.

Questions 44 through 46 refer to this conversation.

W: John, how many brothers and sisters do you have?

M: I have four brothers and three sisters.

W: Wow, you have a big family! Are you the youngest?

M: No, I have one younger brother.

Questions 47 through 49 refer to this conversation.

W: Tom, what does your brother do?

M: He used to be a doctor, but now he's a fireman.

W: That's amazing. You know, my brother is a fireman, too!

M: Maybe they know each other.

Questions 50 through 52 refer to this conversation.

M: Look at the black clouds. I think it might rain soon.

W: I hope not. I have to walk home.

M: Don't worry. I will give you my umbrella.

W: Thanks. I'll give it back to you in the morning.

Questions 53 through 55 refer to this conversation.

W: I don't have any money. I forgot to bring my wallet.

M: Don't worry. I'll lend you some. Is $50 enough?

W: Thanks, I'll pay you back tomorrow.

Questions 56 through 58 refer to this conversation.

W: Where did you buy that sofa?

M: I didn't. It was a present from my mother.

W: It's a lovely color. I'm looking for something just like it.

M: I'll ask her where she bought it.

Questions 59 through 61 refer to this conversation.

W: Could you pass me my cell phone, please?

M: Sure. Here you go.

W: Thanks. I need to call my friend. I am meeting her after work, but I'm going to be late.

Questions 62 through 64 refer to this conversation.

W: I am going on vacation next week. I need to buy some new clothes.

M: Well, there is a sale at the department store downtown. I think today is the last day.

W: Really? I think I will go and have a look.

M: Yes, maybe you'll find some good bargains.

Questions 65 through 67 refer to this conversation.

M: My cell phone! Where did you find it?

W: It was on my desk. I found it under this file.

M: I have been looking for it for seven days! Didn't you hear it ring?

W: No. I guess the battery has run flat.

Questions 68 through 70 refer to this conversation.

M: Guess what? I quit my job yesterday.

W: Really? Why did you do that?

M: I didn't like my boss. She makes people work too hard. And she never pays overtime.

W: Well, my company is always looking for people. Why don't you apply there?

Part 4

Questions 71 through 73 refer to the following announcement.

M: Attention, shoppers. For the next fifteen minutes, we will have a sale on sweaters in the children's department. Every sweater will be 50% off. Yes, that's right. For just a quarter of an hour, you can buy any child's sweater at just half the original price. Now there is a bargain you can't afford to miss. Hurry now. The clock is ticking.

Questions 74 through 76 refer to the following announcement.

W: The next stop is Main Street. The exit doors are on the left side. You can transfer to the white line, line number 4, to Seoul soccer stadium. Please be careful as you leave the train.

Questions 77 through 79 refer to the following notice.

M: A small dog was lost in the city center two days ago. It is brown with white paws and answers to the name Sam. It was wearing a brown collar. A reward of fifty dollars will be given for help in finding him. Please contact Brian at 655-7951.

Questions 80 through 82 refer to the following talk.

W: Last week, my company went whitewater rafting. It was great fun. There were ten of us in the raft. When I fell in, everyone thought it was very funny. Afterwards, we went to a restaurant and had some Mexican food. It was a very enjoyable day.

Questions 83 through 85 refer to the following talk.

W: Monday will be warm in most areas, with some rain in the north of the country. Temperatures will reach up to 25 degrees in the south and around 20 degrees in the north. Tuesday will also have similar conditions, with slightly higher temperatures of about 23 degrees in the north.

Questions 86 through 88 refer to the following advertisement.

M: Are you trying to improve your English? If so, come to Dave's English camp. We try to make learning English an enjoyable experience for you. We have classes from eight to twelve every morning. After, you can practice speaking with other English students from around the world.

Questions 89 through 91 refer to the following talk.

W: My cousin is a very good photographer. He has spent over three thousand dollars on his camera. He takes pictures of many different things like nature or movie stars. He then sells the pictures to newspapers. He seems to enjoy his job.

Questions 92 through 94 refer to the following talk.

M: Last week, two hundred thousand people ran in the Chicago City Marathon. Over ten million dollars was collected for charity. Most of the money will be given to the city hospital. The winner of the marathon was Karl Muller from Germany, who finished in two and a half hours.

Questions 95 through 97 refer to the following announcement.

M: Attention all students. Due to a burst in the gas pipes, as well as the extremely cold weather, today's classes will be canceled. The school buses will be arriving in twenty minutes to take everyone home. Tomorrow's classes will most likely be canceled also, but the local radio station will make an announcement in the morning.

Questions 98 through 100 refer to the following announcement.

W: Ladies and Gentlemen, we are experiencing some bad weather, so all passengers must return to their seats and fasten their seatbelts. I would like to remind you that this is a non-smoking flight, so smoking will not be permitted. We should pass through the bad weather within thirty minutes, at which time lunch will be served.

Answer Key

Grammar Exercises

1. go
2. has studied
3. seen
4. have
5. been crying
6. plays
7. is running
8. studying
9. finished
10. laughing

Mini Test

Part 1 Picture Description

1. (B) This is a big house.
2. (A) There are boats on the water.
3. (A) The men are working.
4. (C) The man is wearing a tie.
5. (D) The computer is next to the woman.

Part 2 Question and Response

1. (C) He's going to the store.
2. (A) I'll turn on the fan.
3. (B) I'm watching a movie.
4. (B) It's easy. I'll show you.
5. (C) Usually at 8:00.

Part 3 Short Conversations

1. (D) The woman's hair
2. (C) She is making photocopies.
3. (C) The woman is a new employee.
4. (B) The room is dark.
5. (D) She should turn on the lights.
6. (B) The man's sister-in-law

Part 4 Short Talks

1. (A) The subway
2. (B) Fifteen minutes
3. (A) By bus
4. (C) Planning weddings
5. (D) She is planning her sister's wedding.
6. (D) The woman will get married.

Part 5 Incomplete Sentences

1. (C) has lived
2. (B) going
3. (A) belongs
4. (D) at
5. (C) through
6. (A) sometimes
7. (C) have been
8. (B) runs
9. (D) like
10. (A) has been talking
11. (C) are arriving
12. (B) read
13. (B) has
14. (D) been studying
15. (C) clapping

Part 6 Incomplete Texts

1. (C) at
2. (A) notify
3. (C) yet
4. (C) already
5. (B) check
6. (B) sometimes

Part 7 Reading Comprehension

1. (A) Seeing a movie
2. (D) 10%
3. (B) Green Mountain Tea is good for toothaches.
4. (D) Fifty
5. (C) $0.10
6. (A) 98kg
7. (C) 60kg
8. (A) Twice a week
9. (C) In Mexico

••• Unit 2 •••

Grammar Exercises

1. was
2. sold
3. was taking
4. used to
5. finished
6. had been waiting
7. was reading
8. returned
9. borrowed
10. had been waiting

Mini Test

Part 1 Picture Description

1. (D) He is holding the golf clubs.
2. (B) They are washing the dog.
3. (D) The woman is in a hotel room.
4. (B) The man is in a pool.
5. (D) The man is skating.

Part 2 Question and Response

1. (C) To a friend.
2. (A) I was tired.
3. (B) Next Tuesday.
4. (B) You should take a nap.
5. (C) No, it isn't.

Part 3 Short Conversations

1. (B) The man and woman have met before.
2. (D) In a department store
3. (A) He worked in a department store.
4. (B) The man missed a meeting.
5. (C) The traffic was bad.
6. (B) Telephone Eric

Part 4 Short Talks

1. (B) Every year
2. (D) A movie
3. (C) A DVD player and a holiday
4. (A) To help sick people
5. (D) Four weeks
6. (C) It's hard work.

Part 5 Incomplete Sentences

1. (A) was sweeping
2. (D) was
3. (B) had heard
4. (C) had already finished
5. (D) had been raining
6. (C) is flying
7. (B) was built
8. (D) borrows
9. (B) tries on
10. (A) was walking
11. (D) was
12. (C) came
13. (D) in
14. (A) before
15. (D) were counting

Part 6 Incomplete Texts

1. (C) did
2. (C) an appointment
3. (C) patient
4. (B) used to
5. (D) From
6. (C) promise

Part 7 Reading Comprehension

1. (B) Three years old
2. (A) A monitor
3. (B) One cheeseburger and one drink
4. (C) Three months
5. (A) Every year
6. (B) The wife
7. (A) They are moving to Hong Kong.
8. (D) $60
9. (B) She was a Chinese teacher.

Grammar Exercises

1. going
2. to help
3. to travel
4. seeing
5. swimming
6. to buy
7. buying
8. to get
9. smoking
10. going

Mini Test

Part 1 Picture Description

1. (A) This is a meeting room.
2. (A) They have a kite.
3. (B) The girl is next to the dog.
4. (A) The man is singing.
5. (C) The person is painting.

Part 2 Question and Response

1. (B) Great.
2. (B) It was too expensive.
3. (B) Twenty minutes ago.
4. (A) Go shopping.
5. (B) It was very scary.

Part 3 Short Conversations

1. (C) New curtains
2. (D) Green
3. (B) The room will be less stressful.
4. (B) Looking for something
5. (B) On the woman's desk
6. (C) That her glasses are in her car

Part 4 Short Talks

1. (C) Damaged lights
2. (A) One hundred dollars
3. (D) 1000
4. (D) English, Spanish, and French
5. (D) The speaker has a Spanish-speaking friend.
6. (A) English

Part 5 Incomplete Sentences

1. (B) to seeing
2. (D) swimming
3. (B) reminded
4. (C) riding
5. (A) to stretch
6. (B) used to
7. (D) signing
8. (C) take
9. (C) would like
10. (B) combed
11. (D) shopping
12. (B) to finish
13. (D) from
14. (C) to row
15. (C) to look

Part 6 Incomplete Texts

1. (C) call
2. (D) message
3. (B) discuss
4. (C) send
5. (A) complained
6. (D) enjoying

Part 7 Reading Comprehension

1. (B) To the theater
2. (D) Because he's busy
3. (C) The doctor
4. (D) Andy and John
5. (C) Because they wanted to join the army
6. (A) Anyone
7. (B) Two hours
8. (D) Once a week
9. (B) She is not a good singer.

Grammar Exercises

1. are
2. by
3. have
4. is
5. during
6. is
7. have
8. at
9. been
10. were

Mini Test

Part 1 Picture Description

1. (B) They are looking at the book.
2. (A) The birds are on the boat.
3. (A) The men are skiing.
4. (C) The man is reading a newspaper.
5. (C) The people are running.

Part 2 Question and Response

1. (A) At three thirty.
2. (B) I'm fifteen.
3. (B) Yes, I do.
4. (B) To the supermarket.
5. (C) Because it's cold.

Part 3 Short Conversations

1. (A) Use the computer
2. (B) Save documents
3. (D) A presentation
4. (D) At a travel agency
5. (C) A ticket to Los Angeles
6. (B) The ticket is too expensive.

Part 4 Short Talks

1. (C) At 7:15
2. (D) 22A
3. (D) From Spain to Ireland
4. (B) To the people's right
5. (D) Sixteen years
6. (D) Ten

Part 5 Incomplete Sentences

1. (C) employer
2. (C) were
3. (D) during
4. (D) at
5. (C) lend
6. (A) to dance
7. (B) are
8. (C) didn't have
9. (D) went
10. (D) A number of
11. (B) by
12. (D) was
13. (A) were
14. (B) effort
15. (A) by

Part 6 Incomplete texts

1. (B) presentation
2. (C) speaking
3. (A) attend
4. (C) is
5. (B) use
6. (C) each

Part 7 Reading Comprehension

1. (B) To sell old cars
2. (D) Six years old
3. (C) A book and two CDs
4. (C) Ten years
5. (D) Three times a week
6. (C) At a toy company
7. (B) In one month
8. (A) Call her
9. (A) Jenny will visit Sarah next month.

Grammar Exercises

1. clean
2. be able to
3. can
4. ought not to
5. take a good rest
6. Would
7. better not
8. so can
9. will not
10. don't have to

Mini Test

Part 1 Picture Description

1. (A) They are singing.
2. (B) The cow is eating the grass.
3. (B) The couple is camping.
4. (B) The food is on the table.
5. (A) These are gifts.

Part 2 Question and Response

1. (C) I'm leaving at eight o'clock.
2. (B) That's a good idea!
3. (A) I agree.
4. (C) No, she isn't.
5. (C) She's a doctor.

Part 3 Short Conversations

1. (B) To the post office
2. (A) No more than ten minutes
3. (B) In sixty minutes
4. (C) To the store
5. (C) Some eggs
6. (C) Three

Part 4 Short Talks

1. (D) It doesn't feel like a job to him.
2. (C) In the theater
3. (A) His cousin
4. (C) People with old cell phones
5. (D) On the weekend
6. (D) Crazy

Part 5 Incomplete Sentences

1. (A) will
2. (A) go
3. (A) should not
4. (D) arrives
5. (D) bring
6. (A) ought not to
7. (B) rather not go
8. (A) already
9. (C) be able to
10. (A) on
11. (A) Would
12. (A) to go shopping
13. (D) tell
14. (A) in
15. (B) by

Part 6 Incomplete Texts

1. (A) tell
2. (B) could
3. (C) before
4. (A) time
5. (D) could
6. (C) were

Part 7 Reading Comprehension

1. (A) A television
2. (D) For fourteen days
3. (B) In the country
4. (D) Ride horses
5. (A) How to make cookies
6. (C) Singapore
7. (A) Beijing
8. (C) Jakarta
9. (B) Because she is taking a trip

Grammar Exercises

1. who
2. that
3. whose
4. another
5. that
6. who
7. in which
8. on which
9. where
10. why

Mini Test

Part 1 Picture Description

1. (D) The teddy bear is next to the box.
2. (A) They are having a car race.
3. (C) These are two parrots.
4. (A) The man is looking at the list.
5. (C) The woman is playing golf.

Part 2 Question and Response

1. (A) Next Tuesday.
2. (B) Not yet.
3. (B) He's from Chicago.
4. (A) Yes, they're very nice.
5. (A) Here, have some cookies.

Part 3 Short Conversations

1. (A) On the telephone
2. (C) When the store is open
3. (A) Ten o'clock
4. (D) Blue
5. (C) His mother
6. (D) She doesn't know where they are.

Part 4 Short Talks

1. (A) Lonely
2. (C) She didn't like the weather.
3. (C) She has lots of friends and things to do.
4. (C) Last year
5. (D) Faster and stronger
6. (D) None of the above

Part 5 Incomplete Sentences

1. (B) that
2. (D) where
3. (C) to whom
4. (D) another
5. (B) see
6. (A) whose
7. (B) which
8. (B) fun
9. (B) that
10. (C) effect
11. (C) on which
12. (A) remind
13. (B) by
14. (D) been
15. (C) with

Part 6 Incomplete Texts

1. (C) that
2. (D) with
3. (A) more
4. (C) sending
5. (A) at
6. (C) why

Part 7 Reading Comprehension

1. (B) Michael's mother
2. (C) Clean his room
3. (B) Science
4. (D) They like their teacher.
5. (B) Physical education
6. (B) April 5th
7. (D) Children under eight years
8. (C) A man and a woman
9. (A) Lifeguards should watch the volleyball competition.

Grammar Exercises

1. furniture
2. batteries
3. doesn't
4. luggage
5. kind
6. is
7. reception
8. people
9. few
10. mail

Mini Test

Part 1 Picture Description

1. (D) The girls are smiling.
2. (A) This is a father and two daughters.
3. (C) This is a beach.
4. (B) These are flowers.
5. (C) They are in a hospital.

Part 2 Question and Response

1. (B) It's the twentieth.
2. (B) Yes, we did.
3. (C) No, thank you.
4. (A) I took the bus.
5. (A) At four o'clock.

Part 3 Short Conversations

1. (D) The manager
2. (D) A red dress and a black jacket
3. (C) He thought Mary would look older.
4. (B) Going on a picnic
5. (A) If she needs to bring anything
6. (A) The following morning

Part 4 Short Talks

1. (B) The food
2. (D) Economics and Korean
3. (D) Madrid, next February
4. (D) A car is blocking the entrance.
5. (B) ST 4571
6. (B) Go to the parking lot

Part 5 Incomplete Sentences

1. (D) the toothpaste
2. (B) my
3. (D) any
4. (C) myself
5. (A) much
6. (B) when
7. (B) slices of bread
8. (C) a few
9. (A) it
10. (C) took
11. (C) the other
12. (A) Can
13. (B) people
14. (A) Jogging
15. (B) with

Part 6 Incomplete Texts

1. (A) chance
2. (C) ready
3. (B) at
4. (A) our
5. (B) open
6. (A) decided

Part 7 Reading Comprehension

1. (B) She has brown spots.
2. (D) If you find Potato Chip
3. (C) The meeting will be on Friday.
4. (D) A free ticket for a friend
5. (C) 300
6. (C) White, green, blue
7. (D) Six
8. (D) Blue
9. (B) Because she is a regular customer

Grammar Exercises

1. heavily
2. frequently
3. hardly
4. to
5. surprisingly
6. violent
7. to walk
8. both
9. that
10. of

Mini Test

Part 1 Picture Description

1. (D) This is a parade.
2. (D) The man is on the bicycle.
3. (C) The man is standing next to the car.
4. (D) The horse is jumping.
5. (D) They are playing volleyball.

Part 2 Question and Response

1. (C) I'm sorry, I'm broke.
2. (A) Sure, go ahead.
3. (B) How about 2 p.m. tomorrow?
4. (B) I'm interested in buying a T-shirt.
5. (A) It's over there.

Part 3 Short Conversations

1. (B) New York
2. (A) Taking a bus from New Jersey
3. (C) Ten minutes
4. (C) Sara's neighbor
5. (C) Peter has no children.
6. (D) Four

Part 4 Short Talks

1. (C) Korean classes
2. (C) They are fun.
3. (C) Saturday
4. (D) More than twenty years
5. (A) Walk around the zoo
6. (D) The elephant

Part 5 Incomplete Sentences

1. (B) both
2. (B) nice
3. (A) open
4. (D) into
5. (B) hard
6. (A) patient
7. (C) for
8. (D) whose
9. (D) empty
10. (C) have
11. (A) often
12. (B) surprising
13. (A) to
14. (D) for
15. (B) to

Part 6 Incomplete Texts

1. (B) almost
2. (C) chased
3. (A) help
4. (C) into
5. (A) good
6. (D) our

Part 7 Reading Comprehension

1. (C) The Giants, the Yellow Socks, the Tigers, and the Superstars
2. (A) The Superstars
3. (B) At summer camp
4. (A) In a couple of weeks
5. (B) She enjoys it.
6. (A) Tokyo
7. (C) London
8. (C) July 30th
9. (C) $200

Grammar Exercises

1. earlier
2. much
3. to
4. as
5. much
6. fastest
7. the most
8. to
9. more
10. as

Mini Test

Part 1 Picture Description

1. (A) The boy is playing a violin.
2. (C) The couple is dressed for a party.
3. (B) The man is working.
4. (C) They are looking at each other.
5. (D) The couple is in the mountains.

Part 2 Question and Response

1. (C) I just polished them.
2. (A) Fewer than last year.
3. (B) Wait. I'll sweep it.
4. (A) But it's faster than driving.
5. (B) On Sunday.

Part 3 Short Conversations

1. (D) Five cups
2. (B) The woman should drink less coffee.
3. (B) It helps her focus on her work.
4. (A) A party
5. (C) After 10 p.m.
6. (B) She left before he arrived.

Part 4 Short Talks

1. (D) He takes a bus.
2. (A) 6:00
3. (C) Play tennis
4. (B) Vehicles
5. (D) Expensive ones
6. (A) 50% or less

Part 5 Incomplete Sentences

1. (B) than
2. (A) faster
3. (C) expensive
4. (B) deeper
5. (B) more
6. (D) most interesting
7. (A) as
8. (B) faster
9. (A) taller
10. (D) running
11. (C) on which
12. (C) less
13. (B) has
14. (A) on
15. (B) raise

Part 6 Incomplete Texts

1. (C) cheapest
2. (B) most convenient
3. (A) are
4. (C) sooner
5. (A) quicker
6. (D) pay

Part 7 Reading Comprehension

1. (C) O'Byrne's Pub
2. (B) Their parents are getting married.
3. (A) Asia
4. (B) There are more girls from Asia than boys from Australia.
5. (C) 95
6. (D) On the fifth floor
7. (C) A DVD player
8. (A) In the morning
9. (A) To tell customers about changes

Grammar Exercises

1. until
2. quite
3. interesting
4. neither
5. during
6. since
7. so
8. as long as
9. and
10. Although

Mini Test

Part 1 Picture Description

1. (C) They are lying on the grass.
2. (A) The man is holding a brush.
3. (B) This is a phone.
4. (B) These are dice.
5. (A) The man is sitting.

Part 2 Question and Response

1. (C) He plays tennis every day.
2. (A) I saw her last night.
3. (A) There's a movie at eight o'clock.
4. (B) It's five years old.
5. (C) Yes, I have a rabbit.

Part 3 Short Conversations

1. (A) To the bookstore
2. (C) Go straight for one block, then turn left.
3. (A) That it has a wide variety of books
4. (C) Go to the supermarket
5. (D) Some soap
6. (B) He might buy the wrong soap.

Part 4 Short Talks

1. (C) Over ten years
2. (B) His opponent hurt his shoulder.
3. (C) He threw him to the ground.
4. (A) Cooking
5. (D) Tomorrow
6. (B) A new job

Part 5 Incomplete Sentences

1. (B) because
2. (B) If
3. (D) Even though
4. (A) lie
5. (D) reading
6. (C) While
7. (A) or
8. (B) nor
9. (B) lately
10. (D) As soon as
11. (B) so
12. (C) by
13. (B) over
14. (D) could
15. (B) into

Part 6 Incomplete Texts

1. (A) as soon as
2. (C) what
3. (A) most
4. (B) for
5. (A) until
6. (C) back

Part 7 Reading Comprehension

1. (D) A bicycle
2. (B) He promises to take care of the bicycle.
3. (C) Thursday
4. (C) Red-and-blue
5. (A) Six years
6. (A) The garden club
7. (D) To the post office
8. (B) Start dinner
9. (B) Frank

Grammar Exercises

1. terrible
2. really
3. A number of
4. student
5. any
6. very
7. enough money
8. something warm
9. Most
10. such

Mini Test

Part 1 Picture Description
1. (C) The man is holding a rabbit.
2. (B) People are at a café.
3. (C) The man is holding a fish.
4. (A) The beach is near the city.
5. (A) There are umbrellas over the tables.

Part 2 Question and Response
1. (B) It was interesting.
2. (A) Nothing special.
3. (A) Almost.
4. (A) It starts next week.
5. (A) For ten years.

Part 3 Short Conversations
1. (A) 75 cents
2. (C) Five
3. (A) $45
4. (C) At a railway station
5. (D) To Midland
6. (D) The local, because it is cheaper.

Part 4 Short Talks
1. (C) People who find it difficult to relax
2. (A) It gives them more energy.
3. (D) Every day except Monday
4. (A) She loved it.
5. (A) Nobody
6. (C) After her walks

Part 5 Incomplete Sentences
1. (D) good
2. (A) every two weeks
3. (C) a lot of
4. (C) a little
5. (C) to wait
6. (A) so
7. (B) listening
8. (B) a few
9. (A) Most
10. (D) to enjoy
11. (C) more interested
12. (D) some
13. (A) has
14. (B) about
15. (C) either

Part 6 Incomplete Texts
1. (D) Almost
2. (A) enough
3. (A) everyone
4. (C) recent
5. (B) looked
6. (D) this

Part 7 Reading Comprehension
1. (B) December 26th
2. (D) Because of the holidays
3. (C) A chili hotdog
4. (D) $8.00
5. (D) Six
6. (C) Four
7. (B) Tomorrow
8. (D) They should read a chapter.
9. (B) Chat with her friend

••• Unit 12 •••

Grammar Exercises

1. any
2. not
3. never
4. rarely
5. want
6. not to
7. does not
8. not afford
9. barely
10. never

Mini Test

Part 1 Picture Description

1. (C) This is a mouse.
2. (B) The girl is smiling.
3. (D) This is a farm.
4. (B) These are peaches.
5. (B) The woman is in the office.

Part 2 Question and Response

1. (A) Yes, we've met before.
2. (A) Only a little bit.
3. (B) It's six o'clock.
4. (C) Thank you.
5. (B) Of course.

Part 3 Short Conversations

1. (A) Parking a car
2. (A) They wasted a lot of time.
3. (D) Find a parking spot
4. (C) The man was late for their appointment.
5. (D) 3:30 p.m.
6. (A) The man is often late.

Part 4 Short Talks

1. (C) Walk out of the building
2. (D) On the football field
3. (C) Twice a year
4. (C) When they hear the bell
5. (D) Their name and class number
6. (C) Three hours

Part 5 Incomplete Sentences

1. (D) climbs
2. (C) not walking
3. (B) no
4. (D) so
5. (A) will never
6. (C) exploded
7. (A) Not wearing
8. (D) than
9. (A) plays
10. (D) does not
11. (A) to buy
12. (C) Not all
13. (B) used
14. (B) of
15. (A) could hardly

Part 6 Incomplete Texts

1. (A) about
2. (D) not to
3. (C) had not
4. (B) of
5. (C) our
6. (A) help

Part 7 Reading Comprehension

1. (A) Columbian coffee
2. (C) $4.00
3. (C) 4:00 p.m.
4. (B) Room 304
5. (D) Ayres Hall
6. (D) April
7. (C) Two
8. (B) Photos
9. (A) At work

Part 1

1. (B) This is a keyboard.
2. (C) The people are watching a show.
3. (A) This is a boat.
4. (C) The women are dancing.
5. (A) The woman is talking on the phone.
6. (D) The car is in front of the house.
7. (A) The people are reading the menu.
8. (A) People are in the swimming pool.
9. (B) The man is sitting next to the table.
10. (A) The man is riding a jet ski.

Part 2

11. (A) I'm sorry, I'll turn it off.
12. (C) 555-3481.
13. (A) Yes, I'd like that.
14. (C) At seven o'clock.
15. (B) No, not yet.
16. (C) Yes, I do.
17. (A) You're welcome.
18. (B) No, we don't.
19. (A) It's next to the bank.
20. (C) No, it's too cold.
21. (B) They're going downtown.
22. (A) I got a bicycle.
23. (B) No, I didn't.
24. (C) Not at all.
25. (A) He's got a cold.
26. (A) It was easy.
27. (B) Would you like a piece?
28. (B) Yes, I bought it yesterday.
29. (C) No problem.
30. (A) I agree.
31. (B) Yes, it's on the sofa.
32. (B) I went to a party.
33. (A) It's downtown.
34. (C) You take the number ten.
35. (A) Sure.
36. (C) I'm going with my family.
37. (B) I usually go after work.
38. (C) I will buy a new cell phone.
39. (B) I will be working at the bank.
40. (B) I didn't have time.

Part 3

41. (B) To attend a conference
42. (C) New York
43. (A) Tuesday
44. (C) Three
45. (D) Eight
46. (A) None
47. (C) He's a fireman.

48. (D) Her brother is a fireman, too.
49. (B) Tom's brother knows the woman's brother.
50. (B) There are a lot of black clouds.
51. (C) She doesn't have an umbrella.
52. (A) Lend the woman an umbrella.
53. (C) She forgot her wallet.
54. (C) $50
55. (C) Tomorrow
56. (D) A sofa
57. (B) The color of his sofa
58. (A) Ask his mother for some information
59. (A) Her cell phone
60. (C) Her friend
61. (B) She is going to be late.
62. (C) Next week
63. (B) New clothes
64. (C) At a department store
65. (D) His cell phone
66. (B) Under a file
67. (C) The battery was dead.
68. (B) He quit his job.
69. (B) She is surprised.
70. (D) The man will look for a new job.

Part 4

71. (B) In a department store
72. (D) $25
73. (C) Parents
74. (C) Main Street
75. (C) The white line
76. (B) Number four
77. (C) In the city center
78. (B) Brown with white paws
79. (D) Fifty dollars
80. (A) Ten
81. (A) A Mexican restaurant
82. (C) He thought it was great fun.
83. (C) In the north
84. (B) 23 degrees
85. (C) There will be some higher temperatures on Tuesday.
86. (B) To make English fun
87. (D) From 8-12
88. (B) Practice speaking English
89. (A) He takes pictures.
90. (C) Over three thousand dollars
91. (C) Newspapers
92. (C) Two hundred thousand
93. (D) To the city hospital
94. (B) Two hours, thirty minutes
95. (B) There is a problem with the heating system.
96. (A) In twenty minutes
97. (D) The local radio station will make an

announcement.

98. (C) On an airplane
99. (D) They are passing through some rough weather.
100. (D) Lunch will be served.

Part 5

101. (A) her
102. (C) feeling
103. (C) They're
104. (B) many
105. (C) to drink
106. (B) some
107. (A) any
108. (B) beautiful
109. (B) works
110. (A) for
111. (D) does
112. (C) by
113. (A) Swimming
114. (B) doing
115. (A) a
116. (A) take
117. (C) need
118. (B) as
119. (C) hiking
120. (B) for
121. (A) broke
122. (C) interesting
123. (D) for
124. (A) who
125. (D) to travel
126. (D) Many of
127. (B) any
128. (C) yet
129. (A) takes
130. (B) hard
131. (B) has
132. (A) on
133. (D) did
134. (B) made
135. (D) for
136. (A) Do
137. (C) orange
138. (B) these
139. (D) drinks
140. (A) play

Part 6

141. (C) your
142. (B) to
143. (B) some
144. (B) about
145. (A) everyone
146. (C) tell
147. (B) what
148. (B) All

149. (B) directly
150. (B) informed
151. (C) no more
152. (A) which

Part 7

153. (D) Next to a highway
154. (C) In winter
155. (C) In a hotel
156. (B) First by airplane, then by taxi, then by bus, then by boat
157. (A) People who are often tired
158. (B) Because it has vitamins
159. (A) You have to take vitamin pills with Vitagetic.
160. (A) In the blue bin
161. (C) Magazines
162. (A) Newspapers
163. (C) On the Internet
164. (A) A Michael Jackson concert
165. (C) $50
166. (D) Chinese food
167. (D) Sunday
168. (C) 56 West Sycamore Street
169. (B) One hour and fifteen minutes
170. (C) In the city
171. (A) In the morning and in the afternoon
172. (D) Twelve and a half hours
173. (A) His new house
174. (D) Three bedrooms
175. (B) A flower garden
176. (D) In February
177. (A) On the fourth floor
178. (D) To the second floor
179. (A) To the fifth floor
180. (B) The store will be relocating.
181. (D) Music 11
182. (C) Science 11
183. (D) English 11 and Art 11
184. (C) It is much better than last year.
185. (A) They think she will not be accepted by a good university.
186. (C) 150 dollars
187. (C) By email and telephone
188. (B) In a daily newspaper
189. (D) Just the sofa
190. (B) He will use his truck.
191. (B) She was sick.
192. (C) Discuss a play
193. (A) A student in Brittany's English class
194. (D) Brittany and Jennifer's English teacher
195. (C) There is a lot of homework for the next class.
196. (C) People who have worked in restaurants before
197. (C) Eight
198. (A) Manager
199. (C) Ten years
200. (C) Mike wants to be manager at Giorgio's Pizza House.

ANSWER SHEET

PRACTICE TEST

LISTENING (Parts 1 - 4)

NO.	ANSWER	NO.	ANSWER	NO.	ANSWER	NO.	ANSWER	NO.	ANSWER
	A B C D		A B C D		A B C D		A B C D		A B C D
1	ⓐ ⓑ ⓒ ⓓ	21	ⓐ ⓑ ⓒ ⓓ	41	ⓐ ⓑ ⓒ ⓓ	61	ⓐ ⓑ ⓒ ⓓ	81	ⓐ ⓑ ⓒ ⓓ
2	ⓐ ⓑ ⓒ ⓓ	22	ⓐ ⓑ ⓒ ⓓ	42	ⓐ ⓑ ⓒ ⓓ	62	ⓐ ⓑ ⓒ ⓓ	82	ⓐ ⓑ ⓒ ⓓ
3	ⓐ ⓑ ⓒ ⓓ	23	ⓐ ⓑ ⓒ ⓓ	43	ⓐ ⓑ ⓒ ⓓ	63	ⓐ ⓑ ⓒ ⓓ	83	ⓐ ⓑ ⓒ ⓓ
4	ⓐ ⓑ ⓒ ⓓ	24	ⓐ ⓑ ⓒ ⓓ	44	ⓐ ⓑ ⓒ ⓓ	64	ⓐ ⓑ ⓒ ⓓ	84	ⓐ ⓑ ⓒ ⓓ
5	ⓐ ⓑ ⓒ ⓓ	25	ⓐ ⓑ ⓒ ⓓ	45	ⓐ ⓑ ⓒ ⓓ	65	ⓐ ⓑ ⓒ ⓓ	85	ⓐ ⓑ ⓒ ⓓ
6	ⓐ ⓑ ⓒ ⓓ	26	ⓐ ⓑ ⓒ ⓓ	46	ⓐ ⓑ ⓒ ⓓ	66	ⓐ ⓑ ⓒ ⓓ	86	ⓐ ⓑ ⓒ ⓓ
7	ⓐ ⓑ ⓒ ⓓ	27	ⓐ ⓑ ⓒ ⓓ	47	ⓐ ⓑ ⓒ ⓓ	67	ⓐ ⓑ ⓒ ⓓ	87	ⓐ ⓑ ⓒ ⓓ
8	ⓐ ⓑ ⓒ ⓓ	28	ⓐ ⓑ ⓒ ⓓ	48	ⓐ ⓑ ⓒ ⓓ	68	ⓐ ⓑ ⓒ ⓓ	88	ⓐ ⓑ ⓒ ⓓ
9	ⓐ ⓑ ⓒ ⓓ	29	ⓐ ⓑ ⓒ ⓓ	49	ⓐ ⓑ ⓒ ⓓ	69	ⓐ ⓑ ⓒ ⓓ	89	ⓐ ⓑ ⓒ ⓓ
10	ⓐ ⓑ ⓒ ⓓ	30	ⓐ ⓑ ⓒ ⓓ	50	ⓐ ⓑ ⓒ ⓓ	70	ⓐ ⓑ ⓒ ⓓ	90	ⓐ ⓑ ⓒ ⓓ
11	ⓐ ⓑ ⓒ ⓓ	31	ⓐ ⓑ ⓒ ⓓ	51	ⓐ ⓑ ⓒ ⓓ	71	ⓐ ⓑ ⓒ ⓓ	91	ⓐ ⓑ ⓒ ⓓ
12	ⓐ ⓑ ⓒ ⓓ	32	ⓐ ⓑ ⓒ ⓓ	52	ⓐ ⓑ ⓒ ⓓ	72	ⓐ ⓑ ⓒ ⓓ	92	ⓐ ⓑ ⓒ ⓓ
13	ⓐ ⓑ ⓒ ⓓ	33	ⓐ ⓑ ⓒ ⓓ	53	ⓐ ⓑ ⓒ ⓓ	73	ⓐ ⓑ ⓒ ⓓ	93	ⓐ ⓑ ⓒ ⓓ
14	ⓐ ⓑ ⓒ ⓓ	34	ⓐ ⓑ ⓒ ⓓ	54	ⓐ ⓑ ⓒ ⓓ	74	ⓐ ⓑ ⓒ ⓓ	94	ⓐ ⓑ ⓒ ⓓ
15	ⓐ ⓑ ⓒ ⓓ	35	ⓐ ⓑ ⓒ ⓓ	55	ⓐ ⓑ ⓒ ⓓ	75	ⓐ ⓑ ⓒ ⓓ	95	ⓐ ⓑ ⓒ ⓓ
16	ⓐ ⓑ ⓒ ⓓ	36	ⓐ ⓑ ⓒ ⓓ	56	ⓐ ⓑ ⓒ ⓓ	76	ⓐ ⓑ ⓒ ⓓ	96	ⓐ ⓑ ⓒ ⓓ
17	ⓐ ⓑ ⓒ ⓓ	37	ⓐ ⓑ ⓒ ⓓ	57	ⓐ ⓑ ⓒ ⓓ	77	ⓐ ⓑ ⓒ ⓓ	97	ⓐ ⓑ ⓒ ⓓ
18	ⓐ ⓑ ⓒ ⓓ	38	ⓐ ⓑ ⓒ ⓓ	58	ⓐ ⓑ ⓒ ⓓ	78	ⓐ ⓑ ⓒ ⓓ	98	ⓐ ⓑ ⓒ ⓓ
19	ⓐ ⓑ ⓒ ⓓ	39	ⓐ ⓑ ⓒ ⓓ	59	ⓐ ⓑ ⓒ ⓓ	79	ⓐ ⓑ ⓒ ⓓ	99	ⓐ ⓑ ⓒ ⓓ
20	ⓐ ⓑ ⓒ ⓓ	40	ⓐ ⓑ ⓒ ⓓ	60	ⓐ ⓑ ⓒ ⓓ	80	ⓐ ⓑ ⓒ ⓓ	100	ⓐ ⓑ ⓒ ⓓ

READING (Parts 5 - 7)

NO.	ANSWER	NO.	ANSWER	NO.	ANSWER	NO.	ANSWER	NO.	ANSWER
	A B C D		A B C D		A B C D		A B C D		A B C D
101	ⓐ ⓑ ⓒ ⓓ	121	ⓐ ⓑ ⓒ ⓓ	141	ⓐ ⓑ ⓒ ⓓ	161	ⓐ ⓑ ⓒ ⓓ	181	ⓐ ⓑ ⓒ ⓓ
102	ⓐ ⓑ ⓒ ⓓ	122	ⓐ ⓑ ⓒ ⓓ	142	ⓐ ⓑ ⓒ ⓓ	162	ⓐ ⓑ ⓒ ⓓ	182	ⓐ ⓑ ⓒ ⓓ
103	ⓐ ⓑ ⓒ ⓓ	123	ⓐ ⓑ ⓒ ⓓ	143	ⓐ ⓑ ⓒ ⓓ	163	ⓐ ⓑ ⓒ ⓓ	183	ⓐ ⓑ ⓒ ⓓ
104	ⓐ ⓑ ⓒ ⓓ	124	ⓐ ⓑ ⓒ ⓓ	144	ⓐ ⓑ ⓒ ⓓ	164	ⓐ ⓑ ⓒ ⓓ	184	ⓐ ⓑ ⓒ ⓓ
105	ⓐ ⓑ ⓒ ⓓ	125	ⓐ ⓑ ⓒ ⓓ	145	ⓐ ⓑ ⓒ ⓓ	165	ⓐ ⓑ ⓒ ⓓ	185	ⓐ ⓑ ⓒ ⓓ
106	ⓐ ⓑ ⓒ ⓓ	126	ⓐ ⓑ ⓒ ⓓ	146	ⓐ ⓑ ⓒ ⓓ	166	ⓐ ⓑ ⓒ ⓓ	186	ⓐ ⓑ ⓒ ⓓ
107	ⓐ ⓑ ⓒ ⓓ	127	ⓐ ⓑ ⓒ ⓓ	147	ⓐ ⓑ ⓒ ⓓ	167	ⓐ ⓑ ⓒ ⓓ	187	ⓐ ⓑ ⓒ ⓓ
108	ⓐ ⓑ ⓒ ⓓ	128	ⓐ ⓑ ⓒ ⓓ	148	ⓐ ⓑ ⓒ ⓓ	168	ⓐ ⓑ ⓒ ⓓ	188	ⓐ ⓑ ⓒ ⓓ
109	ⓐ ⓑ ⓒ ⓓ	129	ⓐ ⓑ ⓒ ⓓ	149	ⓐ ⓑ ⓒ ⓓ	169	ⓐ ⓑ ⓒ ⓓ	189	ⓐ ⓑ ⓒ ⓓ
110	ⓐ ⓑ ⓒ ⓓ	130	ⓐ ⓑ ⓒ ⓓ	150	ⓐ ⓑ ⓒ ⓓ	170	ⓐ ⓑ ⓒ ⓓ	190	ⓐ ⓑ ⓒ ⓓ
111	ⓐ ⓑ ⓒ ⓓ	131	ⓐ ⓑ ⓒ ⓓ	151	ⓐ ⓑ ⓒ ⓓ	171	ⓐ ⓑ ⓒ ⓓ	191	ⓐ ⓑ ⓒ ⓓ
112	ⓐ ⓑ ⓒ ⓓ	132	ⓐ ⓑ ⓒ ⓓ	152	ⓐ ⓑ ⓒ ⓓ	172	ⓐ ⓑ ⓒ ⓓ	192	ⓐ ⓑ ⓒ ⓓ
113	ⓐ ⓑ ⓒ ⓓ	133	ⓐ ⓑ ⓒ ⓓ	153	ⓐ ⓑ ⓒ ⓓ	173	ⓐ ⓑ ⓒ ⓓ	193	ⓐ ⓑ ⓒ ⓓ
114	ⓐ ⓑ ⓒ ⓓ	134	ⓐ ⓑ ⓒ ⓓ	154	ⓐ ⓑ ⓒ ⓓ	174	ⓐ ⓑ ⓒ ⓓ	194	ⓐ ⓑ ⓒ ⓓ
115	ⓐ ⓑ ⓒ ⓓ	135	ⓐ ⓑ ⓒ ⓓ	155	ⓐ ⓑ ⓒ ⓓ	175	ⓐ ⓑ ⓒ ⓓ	195	ⓐ ⓑ ⓒ ⓓ
116	ⓐ ⓑ ⓒ ⓓ	136	ⓐ ⓑ ⓒ ⓓ	156	ⓐ ⓑ ⓒ ⓓ	176	ⓐ ⓑ ⓒ ⓓ	196	ⓐ ⓑ ⓒ ⓓ
117	ⓐ ⓑ ⓒ ⓓ	137	ⓐ ⓑ ⓒ ⓓ	157	ⓐ ⓑ ⓒ ⓓ	177	ⓐ ⓑ ⓒ ⓓ	197	ⓐ ⓑ ⓒ ⓓ
118	ⓐ ⓑ ⓒ ⓓ	138	ⓐ ⓑ ⓒ ⓓ	158	ⓐ ⓑ ⓒ ⓓ	178	ⓐ ⓑ ⓒ ⓓ	198	ⓐ ⓑ ⓒ ⓓ
119	ⓐ ⓑ ⓒ ⓓ	139	ⓐ ⓑ ⓒ ⓓ	159	ⓐ ⓑ ⓒ ⓓ	179	ⓐ ⓑ ⓒ ⓓ	199	ⓐ ⓑ ⓒ ⓓ
120	ⓐ ⓑ ⓒ ⓓ	140	ⓐ ⓑ ⓒ ⓓ	160	ⓐ ⓑ ⓒ ⓓ	180	ⓐ ⓑ ⓒ ⓓ	200	ⓐ ⓑ ⓒ ⓓ